DAVE

Life in music

Douglas Loring Miller

TABLE OF CONTENTS

CHAPTER 1: DNA DOESN'T LIE

CHAPTER 2: YOU'D BETTER BE GOOD

CHAPTER 3: SURE, I WANNA BE YOUR DOG!

CHAPTER 4: EVERY DAY IS A BLANK PAGE

CHAPTER 5: IT'S A FOREVER THING

CHAPTER 6: THE DIVIDE

CHAPTER 7: THE HEARTBREAKER

CHAPTER 8: SWEET VIRGINIA

CHAPTER 9: THIS IS WHAT I WANTED

CHAPTER 10: DOWN UNDER DUI

CHAPTER 11: LIFE WAS PICKING UP SPEED

CHAPTER 12: SWING DANCING WITH AC/DC

CHAPTER 13: INSPIRED, YET AGAIN

CONCLUSION: ANOTHER STEP IN THE CROSSWALK

CHAPTER 1
DNA DOESN'T LIE

"Dad, I want to learn how to play the drums."

I was expecting this. Harper, my eight-year-old daughter, stood there hesitantly holding a pair of my shattered drumsticks in her tiny little hands, peering at me with her large brown eyes like Cindy Lou Who from How the Grinch Stole Christmas. My middle child, my mini-me, my daughter who looks the most like me. I had expected her to be interested in music at some point, but drums? Talk about an entry-level mailroom job at the bottom of the trough!

"Drums?" I responded by raising my brows.

"Yeah!" she exclaimed, her teeth clenched. I paused for a while, and as an emotional knot formed in my throat, I asked, "Okay... and you want me to teach you?" Shifting in her chequered Vans sneakers, she sheepishly nodded and muttered, "Uh-huh," and an immense smile flooded over me, along with a feeling of fatherly pride. We hugged and made our way upstairs to my office's old drum equipment. This is a memory that I will love forever, like a teary Hallmark moment, the kind that those hyper emotional Super Bowl advertisements are made of (the ones that would leave even the hardest monster truck enthusiast crying in their buffalo chicken dip). I realised as soon as we walked into my office that I had never taken official drum lessons and hence had no idea how to teach someone to play the drums. The closest I'd gotten to systematic music tuition was a few hours with an incredible jazz drummer named Lenny Robinson, whom I used to see perform every Sunday afternoon at a local Washington, DC jazz club called One Step Down. One Step Down, a tiny old club on Pennsylvania Avenue just outside of Georgetown, not only hosted established touring acts but also hosted a jazz workshop every weekend, where the house band (led by DC jazz legend Lawrence Wheatley) would perform a few sets and then invite up-and-coming musicians to jam with them onstage. Those courses became a Sunday habit for my mother and me when I was a teenager in the 1980s. We'd sit at a small table, ordering drinks and appetisers and listening to these musical artists play for hours, soaking up the wonderful, improvisational freedom of traditional jazz. Within the stark brick walls, smoke hung in the air, and songs from the small stage were the only sound (talking was strictly prohibited). I was fifteen years old at the time, deep in the throes of my punk rock addiction, listening solely to the fastest, noisiest music I could find, but I somehow connected to the emotional qualities of jazz. Unlike the conventions of modern music (which I despised at the time, like the boy from The Omen at church), I found beauty and vitality in the chaotic tapestry of jazz composition. Sometimes it's structured, sometimes it's not. But, above all, I admired Lenny Robinson's drumming. This was something I'd never seen at a punk rock event before. He made it all look so easy (I now know it's not) with his thunderous attitude and graceful perfection. For me, it was a musical awakening. I'd learned to play the drums by ear on unclean pillows in my bedroom and had never had somebody standing over me telling me what was "right" or "wrong," so my drumming was wild, with irregularity and feral behaviours. I WAS THE MUPPETS' ANIMAL WITHOUT THE CHOPS. Lenny was definitely trained, and I was impressed by his feel and control. My punk rock records were my "teachers" back then: rapid, discordant, screaming slabs of noisy vinyl with drummers who most would not consider traditional, but their crude brilliance was unmistakable, and I will always be grateful to these unsung giants of the underground punk rock scene. Drummers such as Ivor Hanson, Earl Hudson, Jeff Nelson, Bill Stevenson, Reed Mullin, D. H. Peligro, John Wright, etc. To this day, you can hear echoes of their work in my music, with songs like "Song for the Dead" by Queens of the Stone Age, "Monkey Wrench" by Foo Fighters, and even Nirvana's "Smells Like Teen Spirit" (to name a few). All of those musicians appeared to be worlds apart from Lenny's scene, but they all shared the same sensation of beautiful, controlled chaos that I enjoyed every Sunday at One Step Down. That's what I worked hard for. My mother and I decided to celebrate her birthday by attending another weekly jazz workshop at the club one sultry July day. It rapidly became our "thing," and it's something I remember fondly even now. None of my other friends hung out with their parents, certainly not at a fucking jazz club in downtown DC, so it made me think she was inherently awesome and that this was just another way to build our friendship. We were truly friends in the age of Generation X, divorce, and dysfunction. They still are! My mother went to me after a few baskets of fries and a few sets from Lawrence Wheatley's quartet and asked, "David, would you go up and sit in with the band as a birthday present to me?" I don't remember precisely what my first reaction was, but it was probably something along the lines of "ARE YOU OUT OF YOUR FUCKING MIND?" I mean, I'd only been playing the drums (pillows) for a few years, and having learned from my collection of old, scratched punk rock records, I wasn't anywhere NEAR ready to step up and play JAZZ with these badasses. This was an incredible, unfathomable request. This was going to be fed to the lions. This was a recipe for disaster. But... she was also my mother, and she'd been gracious enough to bring me here in the first place. So . . . I reluctantly consented and carefully rose from our small table, threading my way through the crowded gathering of jazz fans to the coffee-stained sign-up page near the stage. It was divided into two columns: "Name" and "Instrument." I skimmed over the names of other seemingly competent musicians on the list and hastily scribbled "David Grohl—drums." I felt as if I had signed my own death warrant. In a haze, I staggered back to our table, feeling all eyes on me as I sat down and immediately began sweating through my ripped jeans and punk rock T-shirt. What on earth had I just done? Nothing positive could ever come from this! The minutes appeared to stretch into hours as musician after incredible artist was sent to delight those hallowed walls and hardened ears. They could all get along just fine with those jazz cats. With each passing second, my confidence dwindled. My stomach was in knots, my palms were sweating, and my pulse was pounding as I sat trying to follow the band's mind-bending time signatures, wondering how on earth I could ever keep up with the amazing instrumentalists who graced this stage every week. Please don't let me be the next one, I prayed. God, please... Soon after, Lawrence Wheatley's rich baritone drawl blared over the PA speakers, announcing the terrifying words that still haunt me to this day: "Ladies and gentlemen, please welcome... on the drums... David Grohl."

I nervously stood to a scattering of applause, which rapidly faded as the audience realised I wasn't a seasoned jazz star, but rather a skinny suburban punk with strange hair, muddy Converse Chucks, and a T-shirt that screamed KILLING JOKE. The dread on the band's faces as I approached the stage gave the impression that the Grim Reaper himself was on his way. When I walked onto the platform, the great Lenny Robinson handed me his sticks and I hesitantly sat on his throne, and for the first time, I saw the room through his eyes. No longer shielded behind the safety of my mother's snack table, I was now literally in the hot seat, trapped under the stage lights with every audience member's gaze pressing down on me as if to say, "Okay, kid... show us what you've got." The band kicked into something I'd never played before (i.e., any jazz tune ever) with a basic count, and I did my best to merely keep time without dying in a pool of my own vomit. No solo, no flare, just keep the tempo steady and don't mess it up. Fortunately, it was over in a moment (except the vomit) and without issue. Unlike the majority of the other musicians who had performed that day, I had a song that was unusually short (albeit not by accident). Consider this: I walked away with the relief that one receives at the completion of root canal surgery. With a timid smile and an uncomfortable bow, I stood and thanked the band. If the band had only realised what I was up to, they would have comprehended such a desperate act of folly. These poor musicians had unintentionally allowed me to give my mother a birthday gift she would never forget (much to the chagrin of about seventy-five paying customers), which meant more to me than any standing ovation I could have dreamed for. Humbled, I walked back to our hors d'oeuvres table in shame, believing that I had a long, long way to go before I could call myself a true drummer. That fateful afternoon sparked a spark in me. Inspired by my failure, I decided that I needed to learn how to play the drums from someone who knew what they were doing, rather than attempting to figure it out on my bedroom floor all by myself. And there was only one person who could show me how: the great Lenny Robinson. A few Sundays later, my mother and I returned to One Step Down, and I cornered Lenny on his way to the bathroom, my naive bravado barely summoned. "Please excuse me, sir. "Do you teach lessons?" In my best Brady Bunch mumble, I inquired. "Of course, guy. "Thirty dollars per hour," he explained. Thirty dollars an hour? I wondered. That's six lawns I'd have to mow in the oppressive heat of Virginia! That's the equivalent of a weekend's wages at Shakey's Pizza! That's an eighth of an ounce of marijuana I wouldn't be able to smoke this week. DEAL. We swapped phone numbers and agreed on a date. I was on track to become the next Gene Krupa! Or so I had hoped... Our thirteen-hundred-square-foot Springfield home was far too small for a full drum set (hence the impromptu pillow practice set in my tiny bedroom), but for this special occasion I brought in the bottom-of-the-line five-piece Tama kit from my band Dain Bramage's practice space, which was nowhere near Lenny's calibre of gear. As I excitedly awaited his arrival, I uncomfortably positioned the filthy drums in front of the living room stereo and shined them up with some Windex I found under the kitchen sink, thinking that soon all the neighbours would hear him ripping it to tears... and think it was me!

"He's arrived!" He's arrived!" As if Santa Claus had just come into our driveway, I exclaimed. I met him at the door and led him into our small living room, where the drums sat sparkling and reeked of nearly dry glass cleaner. He perched on the stool, studied the instrument, and began blazing those same impossible chords I'd seen so many Sundays at the jazz club, a whirlwind of hands and sticks delivering machine gun drum rolls in perfect rhythm. I couldn't believe it was occurring on the same carpet where I had spent my entire life dreaming of becoming a world-class drummer someday. It was finally happening. This was my fate. I was on my way to becoming the next Lenny Robinson, as his riffs became mine.

"Okay," he said when he was done. "Let's see what you can do."

I erupted into my "greatest hits" montage of riffs and techniques borrowed from all of my punk rock heroes, crashing and shattering that cheap drum set like a hyperactive toddler having a full-fledged tantrum in an explosion of raw, rhythmless magnificence. Lenny watched intently and quickly realised, with a severe expression, how much labour would be required in this gig. He stopped me after a few cacophonous minutes of awful soloing and said, "Okay... first of all... you're holding your sticks backward." The first lesson. I quickly flipped them around to their proper direction, embarrassed, and apologised for such a rookie mistake. I'd always kept them back because I felt the fat end of the stick would make a much louder sound when it hit the drums, which worked well in my style of Neanderthal pummeling. I had no idea it was the polar opposite of proper jazz drumming. I'm a moron. He then demonstrated a conventional hold, taking the stick in my left hand and passing it through my thumb and middle finger, as all true drumming greats had done before him, and certainly before me. This one change utterly destroyed everything I had believed I knew about drumming up until that moment, leaving me crippled behind the kit, as if I were learning to walk after a decade-long coma. He started showing me simple, single-stroke rolls on a practice pad as I strained to keep hold of the stick in this impossible new way. Right-left-right-left. Over and over, slowly hitting the pad to find a constant balance. Right-left-right-left. Again. Right-left-right-left. The class was over before I knew it, and I realized that at thirty dollars an hour, it was probably cheaper for me to go to Johns Hopkins and become a fucking brain surgeon than to learn how to play drums like Lenny Robinson. I gave him the money and thanked him for his time, and that was the end of it. My one and only drum lesson.

"OK... ummm... so this is the kick drum." "Your foot goes there," I replied, pointing to Harper's little sneaker on the bass pedal. "This is your hi-hat; your other foot goes there." She sat down, sticks in hand, ready to catch a whale. I fast-forwarded over all of the confusing right-left-right-left nonsense that Lenny Robinson had shown me (all respect, Lenny) and went straight to teaching her a beat. "Ummm . . . okay . . . here's a simple kick-snare pattern . . ." I stopped her after a few fruitless attempts and said, "Wait. "I'll be right back," I said as I dashed out of the room. I understood exactly what she required. It wasn't my fault. Back in Black by AC/DC was playing. I turned on the title track and told her to pay attention. "Hear that?" I inquired. "That is a kick drum. That concludes the hi-hat. That is the snare drum." She listened intently and then began to play. Her time was impeccable, which any drummer understands is more than half the battle. She had a natural, built-in metre, and once she had the coordination of her motions down, she began playing with incredible feel. As Harper played, I leaped and cheered, my heart swelled with joy, headbanging and singing along with the songs. Then I noticed something odd: her posture. Her broad back arched forward somewhat, sharp arms and narrow elbows angled forward slightly, chin elevated over the snare... and I saw it. SHE WAS A COPY OF ME PLAYING THE DRUMS WHEN SHE WAS HER AGE. I felt like I was time-travelling and having an out-of-body experience at the same time. Not only that, but my grinning doppelganger was learning to play the drums the same way I had thirty-five years before: by listening to music with her mom. But I wasn't entirely surprised. As I already stated, I was always expecting this. As I stated in the foreword to my mother's book, From Cradle to Stage, I believe that these musical impulses are present, lurking somewhere deep within the DNA strand and simply waiting to be awakened.

"DNA is a miraculous thing," I wrote. We all have characteristics of individuals we've never met hidden deep within our chemistry. I'm no scientist, but I believe my musical abilities demonstrate this. There is no supernatural involvement here. This is real human flesh and blood. This is something that comes from within. I knew all I needed was that DNA and a lot of patience (which my mother definitely had in abundance) the day I picked up a guitar and performed Deep Purple's 'Smoke on the Water' by ear. Someone gave birth to these ears, heart, and mind. Someone who shared my passion for music and song. I was given a genetic symphony that was just ready to be performed. It only took that spark."

Harper's "spark" had arrived the day before as she sat in her seat at the Roxy nightclub on Sunset Boulevard, watching her older sister, Violet, perform her debut concert at the tender age of eleven. Yes, I was aware of it as well. Violet was a very talkative child. By three, she was speaking with the fluency and vocabulary of a much older child, frequently startling unsuspecting waiters at restaurants from her booster seat with properly enunciated pleas like "Excuse me, sir?" Could you perhaps provide me with some additional butter for my bread?" (Every time, I nearly peed my pants laughing as I watched folks do a double take as if we were a perverted ventriloquist performance.) When she was throwing a temper tantrum at the dinner table at home, I tried to calm her down by saying, "Look, it's okay, everyone gets angry sometimes." "Even I get angry!" she replied, "I'm not angry! "I'm just irritated!" (I still don't understand the distinction, but Violet does.) I eventually found she had a high aural recall and an excellent sense of pattern recognition, allowing her to accurately reproduce or repeat things by ear. That quickly progressed to doing accents on demand, where she would run through spot-on impersonations of Irish, Scottish, English, Italian, and other people before even getting out of her smoothie-stained car seat.

CHAPTER 2
YOU'D BETTER BE GOOD

"Okay . . . so, you wanna play some Zeppelin or AC/DC or something?"

The iconic guitarist of DC's best hardcore punk rock band, Scream, hunched over in a chair just in front of my drum set was none other than Franz Stahl. As a seventeen-year-old mega-fan, I couldn't stop shivering on my drum stool, my calloused hands gripping my broken drumsticks in white-knuckle eagerness, ready to jam with my personal idol. It was brutally obvious that this strange feeling was not reciprocated. Franz appeared to be as excited about this audition as if it were a trip to the dentist for a double root canal.

"No, man . . . let's do Scream songs!" I almost screamed. He looked up from the guitar in his lap, a little surprised, and asked, "Oh yeah? "Which ones are you familiar with?"

This was the moment I had been looking forward to. I looked Franz in the eyes and boldly said, "I know them all..." in my best Clint Eastwood-esque tone. The gloomy, underlit basement of this Arlington, Virginia, head shop soon erupted in a thunderous avalanche of wailing guitar and stratospheric BPM. Franz and I went through their whole catalogue, album after album, even playing songs that hadn't yet been released to the public (okay, I had a few bootlegs). I could feel Franz's mood lift with each song, as I required little to no direction for any verse, chorus, or finale to guide me. He had no idea that his tunes had become ingrained in my mind. After all, with the exception of one lesson from a local jazz drummer ("You're holding your sticks backward, David"), I'd learned to play the drums primarily by listening to Scream.

My punk rock baptism had happened only a few years before, and I had started collecting records with the ravenous fervour of a crackhead in heat, spending all of my hard-earned money on any album I could find in the hardcore section at Olsson's Books and Records in Georgetown, one of the few local record stores that actually carried underground music. Every penny of my Shakey's pizza and landscaping wages went toward amassing a collection of loud, fast, and beautifully primitive albums, which I would eagerly purchase with crumpled bills and carefully counted coins, racing home to throw them on my turntable, inspecting every detail from the artwork to the credits as I played them on repeat at concert-level volume. My mother was a very tolerant woman who let me listen to whatever music I wanted (including the odd Satanic death metal band).

Scream, on the other hand, was unique. Their musicianship and dynamics were a little deeper and broader than those of most other hardcore bands, allowing them to easily delve into classic rock, metal, ska, and even reggae. More importantly, their songs were full of very captivating melodies that seemed to awaken the Beatles fan in me, which most other punk rock bands had to replace with atonal cacophony due to creative incompetence. In addition, their drummer, Kent Stax, was a primal force of nature. His speed and technique were unrivalled, indicating that he knew more about the drums than most self-taught punk rock drummers. You could tell the dude had practised his paradiddles because he was dressed like Buddy Rich in Doc Martens and a leather jacket. I would sit with my pillows and a pair of large marching band drumsticks, playing along to my Scream records until sweat practically dripped down my bedroom windows, attempting to replicate Kent's lightning-fast drumming, which was no easy chore. I didn't have my own band at the time, let alone a drum kit, but it didn't matter. I could close my eyes and envision myself as Scream's drummer, thrashing away to my favourite songs as if they were my own. Scream were a group of lifelong friends who met in high school and went on to establish one of America's most influential punk bands, and were considerably older than me. They formed in 1979 after witnessing the renowned Bad Brains play in a tiny downtown club called Madam's Organ. They had become local heroes, revered by all musicians in the scene, and I would go see them whenever I could. Lead singer Pete Stahl stalked the stage like a vagabond Jim Morrison, bassist Skeeter Thompson kept the grooves solid, and guitarists Franz Stahl and Harley Davidson (yep, you read that correctly) were a dazzling duo of crisp rhythms and solos. As macabre as it may sound, I used to fantasise about being in the audience at a Scream show and hearing an announcement over the PA system that said, "We apologise for any inconvenience, but

Scream will not be able to perform tonight due to an emergency with their drummer." That is, unless someone in the audience can fill in for him...."—and I would jump up on the drum set and save the day. I know it's juvenile, but hey... a kid can dream...

My skills as an amateur pillow percussionist eventually transcended the limitations of my ten-by-ten bedroom, and I began playing an actual drum kit in legitimate bands, including Freak Baby, Mission Impossible, and Dain Bramage. My abilities were skyrocketing, and I was putting all of the tricks I'd learned from playing along to my favourite songs to good use, finally showing my own bastardised versions of all my favourite drummers. Given my pillow-beating training, the equivalent of sprinting in the sand, I was tremendously heavy-handed when I sat down behind a real drum set. I damaged skins and cymbals at an astounding and terribly expensive pace, so much so that I became a regular at the local music store, continually replacing my shattered gear as the jaded employees joyfully took my money, week after week. I noticed a xeroxed sheet of paper out of the corner of my eye one day as I passed the bulletin board full of flyers and adverts on the wall outside the front door of the music shop. It read: SCREAM LOOKING FOR DRUMMER. TEXT FRANZ.

This couldn't be, I reasoned. To begin with, why would Scream, an internationally known band, advertise for drummer auditions at a run-down music store in Falls Church, Virginia? Second, how could they possibly find a drummer who could even come close to sounding like Kent Stax on their fantastic records? I jotted down the number and decided to call, even if it was just to tell my friends that I had spoken with THE Franz Stahl over the phone. I was seventeen years old, still in high school, and in a band with two of my closest friends called Dain Bramage, so I wasn't qualified or ready to commit to actually joining a band as established as Scream, but I couldn't pass up the chance to at least jam with them once for bragging rights. My silly, childish idea of swooping in and saving the concert had possibly expressed itself in this unexpected turn of events. I knew deep down that I had to let the cosmos take its course. I dashed home and nervously dialled the number from my mother's desk phone, pushing aside the ungraded school papers. To my surprise, Franz answered, and after a stuttering presentation of my fictitious résumé (BS), he told me that the band didn't have anywhere to practise right now, but he'd keep my number and contact me back when they could. I took that as a positive sign and waited for him to respond. Of course, on that first call, I overlooked a few crucial details. The most obvious omission? My age. I couldn't believe he'd allow a seventeen-year-old high school junior who still lived with his mother to try out for his band, so I did what any ambitious young rocker would do: I lied and told him I was twenty-one.

After weeks of not hearing from Franz, I decided to give it one more try, contacting his phone again in the hopes that he had misplaced mine. His girlfriend answered and, after a lengthy conversation, agreed to have him call me. (As my wise old age has taught me, if you want something from a musician, ask their girlfriend.) It worked, and he returned my call within hours. We chose that shabby cellar in Arlington for a time and day. I begged to borrow my sister's 1971 white VW Bug for the evening and amazingly fit my complete drum equipment inside it like thirty clowns playing expert-level Tetris. There was hardly enough room for me to breathe, let alone shift gears as I drove, but nothing was going to stop me from getting to that audition. As I sped down the interstate, my thoughts raced with excitement, seeing myself IN THE SAME ROOM as Pete, Skeeter, Harley, and Franz, blowing their minds with my next-level crap and living out my rock and roll fantasy. When I arrived, I was greeted solely by Franz. Based on my dorky, certainly not twenty-one-year-old voice over the phone, I'm sure he'd warned the others that my audition was most likely a waste of their time and spared them the agony. My hopes for a one-night encounter with the all-powerful Scream were quickly crushed, but that didn't stop me from playing like it was my life depended on it. Because it was true. After that, Franz seemed pleasantly surprised and asked if I wanted to come back and jam again later. I couldn't believe what I was hearing. I had at least made it through round one. I cheerfully consented, painstakingly loaded my drum set back into the VW Bug, and went home with a heart full of pride, feeling like I'd just won the lottery. The following audition was with the entire cast. Franz had apparently told the band that I was worth listening to, and the rest joined in, fascinated to witness this thin, no-name guy from Springfield who knew every one of their songs pound the living shit out of his cheap

Tama drum kit like he was in a stadium full of people. Now I was genuinely barking with the big dogs, surrounded by faces I'd only seen on album sleeves or in the crowd while dancing and singing along at the top of my lungs. The amazing sound of Scream was rocking that dingy basement, yet Kent's rudimental drumming had been replaced with my unrelenting Neanderthal wallop, hardened by years of running in the sand. After each successful rehearsal, I realised that my objective of jamming with Scream for bragging rights was becoming more serious. They all agreed that I was the drummer they were looking for, so I was now faced with the real-life opportunity to join an established band that had made a name for themselves with a killer catalogue, amassed a loyal following, and toured not only across the country but also internationally. My fantasy was becoming a reality.

I WAS STANDING AT A CROSSROADS. With each terrible grade card, my future looked more and more like a life of physical labour and suburban monotony. My heart was completely devoted to music, my one and only passion, therefore my grades (and attendance) had already deteriorated to the point of no return. My mother was a much-loved teacher at our neighbourhood high school, and I, her only son, was speeding down a dead-end street on a collision course with the school guidance counsellor at best, expulsion at worst. Then there was my father, with his fantasies of me becoming a respectable Republican businessman, the most improbable of all scenarios. At this point, I'm sure he'd given up hope for my future on Capitol Hill, but he was my father, and he'd ingrained in me a fear of disappointing him from the start. Dain Bramage was another of my good buddies. I'd known Dave Smith and Reuben Radding for a long time, and our little three-piece made a lot of noise. We hadn't done much touring and hadn't even built up much of a local fan base, but we were a young band giving it our all. In retrospect, I believe we were "before our time," as our sound would have fit nicely into the early-nineties underground explosion, combining the intensity of punk music with the melodies of REM, Mission of Burma, and Hüsker Dü. But we were still kind of floating at the moment. To uproot my life and join Scream would entail abandoning school, much to the chagrin of my public school teacher mother; foregoing the already poor connection I had with my disapproving father; and disbanding the band I had formed with two close friends. To say the least, it was a huge leap of faith with no promise of any type of safety net. It was some shite from the burnt dirt. I just didn't have the courage after much thought and soul searching. Perhaps because I didn't believe in myself. So I respectfully rejected, thanking them, and my life continued as I sped down my dead-end road.

A few months later, I noticed Scream was performing at the 9:30 Club, a Washington, DC icon for underground music. It was a dark, dirty dive pub with a legal capacity of only 199 people, but it was our church, and I had seen dozens of acts there over the years, even playing a few myself. I decided to attend the event since I now regarded the men to be my friends, but I knew it would be sad to witness a band I could have joined but didn't because of fear. Change phobia. The terror of the unknown. The fear of maturing. The house lights were turned out, the band took their seats, and Kent Stax began the walloping snare drum opening to "Walking by Myself," a more recent song that invoked the fire of the Stooges and the MC5 in a wall of guitars and powerful groove. The energy in the packed club was like a tightly wound coil about to burst, and when the entire band kicked in, the place utterly fucked up...

I sang these lines at the top of my lungs, and everything made sense. I immediately regretted missing out on something so cathartic. My heart surged into my throat like it was blasted from a cannon, and I knew right then and there that this was my destiny, my band, my future, and my life. My dead-end suburban life's crossroads dissolved, and I decided to take that leap of faith, leaving everything behind for the emotion that surged through my veins when the two hundred people in that room exploded in a wave of mayhem and excitement. After the show, I informed the band that I had made a blunder and wished to be reinstated. They greeted me with wide arms after some cajoling and assuring them that I was truly dedicated this time. Kent had lately become a parent and had made the decision to devote his life to his family. His decision to take a different road opened up a new one for me. All I had to do now was flip my life upside down. Of course, my main concern was my mother. The woman who had made so many sacrifices for me, devoted every second of her life to my personal well-being, and showed me nothing but love since I was born. I never wanted to let her down since, aside from being my mother, she was also my best friend. I couldn't fail her. I prefer to think of her as disciplining me with freedom by allowing me to wander, discover my way, and eventually find myself. I never wanted to jeopardise her trust, so I always respected her and kept my calm. I knew that my leaving school at such a young age would break her heart, but I also knew that staying would break mine.

We sat at her desk, and I stated, my head bowed in shame, that I intended to drop out of high school and travel the world. Her reaction?

"YOU'D BETTER BE GOOD."

My mother must have known deep down that I was not college material after twenty-five years of teaching underachievers like myself. But she had faith in me. She saw the light in me and realised that my heart, soul, and drive did not come from any blackboard or textbook under the mesmerising hum of the classroom lights. "It's not always the kid who fails school," she used to say. Sometimes the school fails the child." So, as she always did, she let me wander, find my way, and discover myself.

My father, on the other hand, was a different story. My father and the guidance counsellor read the riot act to me in the principal's office, flanked by my parents, and predicted a life of poverty and despair. In their eyes, I was a worthless punk, a hoodlum rat with nothing to offer other than filling their gas tanks on weekends or shining their loafers at the airport while they waited for their next flight, but I sat there and took it all like Rocky Balboa, thinking, Fuck you. I'm going to prove you both wrong. What's my favourite line? "You probably do all the things that a kid your age shouldn't do, like smoke cigarettes and drink coffee." Coffee? When was coffee designated as a class A drug? I proudly admitted to both. As we walked to our separate cars in the parking lot, my father screamed, "AND STAY OFF THE DRUGS!!!" before officially disowning me for good. To this day, it remains the most trembling, Bob Dole-esque display of tight-ass Republican fury I have ever witnessed. I couldn't help but laugh. His deterioration could no longer harm me. I was finally off the hook, and so was he (I recall him driving a new, forest-green Plymouth Volare shortly after I graduated from high school, and I can only assume that the meagre college fund he had set aside for me was immediately withdrawn and blown on this most pimp-ass ride). The cord had been severed, and I was free to flee. I THOUGHT I'D BETTER BE GOOD.

My pals in Dain Bramage, on the other hand... they were irritated. I abandoned them, and primitive voodoo dolls emblazoned with my face may have been impaled over stacks of burning Scream records for years to come, but I am happy to tell you that we are all still friends, and we try to visit each other whenever we can. I Scream Not Coming Down, our sole LP, was recorded in July 1986 during a biblical electrical storm above Crofton, Maryland, and is a temper tantrum of spasmodic rhythm and lovely melody. I shall always be proud of this record, not just because it was my first, but also because of its delightfully distinct qualities. Nobody could compare to us. With my life completely turned upside down, I grabbed a job at a nearby furniture warehouse prepping trucks full of gaudy entertainment centres and recliners for delivery and began regularly practising with Scream. We spent months perfecting our sound and writing new material before making our debut on July 25, 1987, at a benefit show for Amnesty International at Johns Hopkins, which was to be followed by a silent candlelight march past several international embassies to draw attention to human rights abuses around the world. This was the most terrified I'd ever been about performing, not only because of the size of the audience (anything over twelve people was stadium rock to me), but also because the room was packed with all of my hometown idols. Minor Threat, Fugazi, and Rites of Spring all looked on to see if I could fill the enormous shoes of the great Kent Stax, and I felt it was my personal responsibility to make the band proud. After all, Scream was one of their heroes as well.

A fall tour of America, scheduled to begin in October, was planned. Scream had completed this 6,000-mile circle around the country several times before, but this was to be my first, something I had fantasised about since I had picked up my first guitar. The prospect of travelling from town to town with nothing but the burden of rocking you night after night almost seemed too good to be true.

The proposed itinerary read like the back of an old Grand Funk Railroad concert T-shirt, with twenty-three performances in less than a month taking us up the East Coast, across the Midwest, over the Rockies to the West Coast, and back home through the South. I had only traveled away from home once before, to Chicago on one of our big family road trips, so seeing towns like Kansas City, Des Moines, San Francisco, Austin, Tacoma, and Los Angeles on the itinerary simply blew my fucking mind. I was not only overjoyed, but I felt like I was driving there in a Dodge van. Vans have long been the favoured and most cost-effective means of transportation for new, independent bands who need to get from point A to point B with little to no money. All bands, from the Beatles to Bad Brains, start here, or should. The van not only serves as your equipment truck, properly packed to accommodate an entire backline of gear (many amplifiers, guitars, and drums), but it also serves as your home away from home. A place to sleep when there is no hotel room (which there never is), a place to warm up when there is no backstage, and a place to form lifetime friendships with your bandmates on those epic, tight cross-country treks. I can assure you that it is not for everyone. It takes a specific type of person with a certain temperament to endure months in what appears to be a little submarine with wheels, but if you can handle it, it becomes a formative experience that you will eternally rely on for life perspective.

With five members in our band (plus one roadie, none other than my childhood friend Jimmy Swanson), we had to meticulously manage the space in our van. I was the band's youngest member by nearly ten years, and this was to be my first tour, so to say I was green would be an understatement. "Hey!" As we climbed into the van, Harley barked at me from the front seat. "Don't be asking me to pass you stuff from the back every ten seconds, you hear me?" We hadn't even backed out of the goddamned driveway before Ken Kesey's Further began to resemble the river patrol boat from Apocalypse Now. Fuck. I'd finally admitted in an interview a few months ago that I wasn't twenty-one, but just eighteen, having lied about my age on that first contact with Franz. The others had glanced at me in surprise, but we were such a well-oiled rock and roll machine from all of those hot rehearsals in that tiny basement that it didn't matter. There was no going back now. The only problem with my lie was that I wasn't legally allowed inside some of the bars where we were scheduled to play, so we kept our mouths shut, and if anyone ever found out, I'd sit in the van patiently waiting to play, jump onstage when it was time, tear the roof off the joint, then scurry back to the van immediately after the show, drenched in sweat.

On those lengthy rides, we would lie across that squeaky, quaking platform in our musty sleeping bags, reading, listening to music, laughing, farting, and passing the time in whatever way we could. Being confined in such a tight place with so many people for such periods of time really favors the little time you have onstage, because when you finally set up and plug in, you just want to fuck up. Any anguish, frustration, homesickness, or depression you may be feeling is taken out on your instrument in a primitive fit of rage for that brief hour of performance, and it doesn't get any better if you're playing loud rock and roll. CBGB's in New York City was one of the first destinations on that trip. I had only been to New York City once before, on a family trip paid for by my mother taking on an extra job as the JV girls' soccer coach for $400 (it was a miracle of couponing and all-you-can-eat buffets), and I was giddy with anticipation to return, and to the legendary CBGB's no less! This was punk rock's epicentre, the soundtrack of my life, and I'd soon be standing on that same stage, playing my heart out for the ghosts of those who had paved the path for young punks like me. The Ramones, the Cramps, Talking Heads, Television, Patti Smith, Bad Brains—this was holy ground, and the fact that I had made it this far was my life's greatest success.

The sight of the classic awning above the front entrance sent goosebumps down my spine upon arrival. I was stunned by its beauty, weathered and deteriorated from years of dirt in the Bowery, precisely as I had seen in decades of black-and-white images. We fortunately (incredibly) found a parking space immediately in front of the club, bursting out of our van like Jeff Spicoli after hours of smoke and imprisonment. The famed Harley Flanagan, bassist of New York's most renowned band, the Cro-Mags, met us. I was awestruck. Their album The Age of Quarrel was one of my top ten punk albums of all time, and here I was, face to face with the most terrifying punk rocker I'd ever seen. It only took one look at him to realise he shouldn't be played with. Ever. Plus, he had a pit dog on a leash who was almost as ferocious as he was, so I kept my distance until he saw Skeeter and Pete and it suddenly transformed into a reunion of old friends, all smiles and handshakes and mutual respect. I was introduced and must have looked like a schoolgirl at a Beatles concert, meeting a "rock star." We invited Harley to the event, but he rejected due to a lack of space for his dog, so we politely volunteered to keep the dog in our van out front while we played. The issue has been resolved. We began to prepare our equipment for our afternoon position on the bill.

As I nervously set up my drums in front of a packed crowd, I couldn't find my drum key (a vital tool for tuning, tightening, or adjusting any piece of drum hardware) and soon realised that I had left it in the van. "Dude!" I yelled at Pete. I need the keys to the van right away!!" He tossed them to me from across the stage and told me we'd be on in five minutes, so I pushed my way through the mob all the way to the front door and hurried to the vehicle parked out front. I eventually slid the key into the keyhole, flipped the lock, grasped the handle to open the door, and "RAHAHARAHHAHARAHAHAH!!!!!!!" In a furious fit of rage, the face of the most demonic, bloodthirsty pit bull filled the glass, almost making me soil myself. Fuck! I pondered. There was a packed club waiting for us to begin at any moment, and the only thing standing between me and that fucking drum key was a terrifying fifty-pound monster of muscle and teeth. I needed to locate Harley and find him quickly. I dashed back into the club, scanning the dark room for his famous sneer until I located him and begged for his help. When I opened the van door with Harley by my side, I was greeted by an adorable puppy wagging its tail in delight to see its best friend, squealing and licking his face until I found the drum key, locked up again, and made it to the stage in time to tear CBGB's a new asshole. Not only would there have been no show if it hadn't been for Harley Flanagan, but I wouldn't even have a nose or lips right now. We then travelled to the Midwest for gigs in Chicago and Detroit. Of course, I was no stranger to Chicago, but I thought Detroit to be something exotic, undiscovered terrain. Of course, everyone is aware of its rich musical past, but many are unaware that it was America's murder capital during the two years preceding my first visit (rivalled only by Washington, DC), so there wasn't much sightseeing to be done unless it was from the protection of the van. Not only was this one of America's roughest towns, but it was also home to some of America's harshest bands—it's no accident that both the MC5 and the Stooges were from Detroit. Our engagement that night was with Laughing Hyenas at Paycheck's in Hamtramck, a primarily Polish neighbourhood about five miles from downtown Detroit. The Hyenas were as rude and vicious as their moniker would suggest, yet they were gracious enough to offer us to stay at their residence after the event. They lived in a group house in Ann Arbor, which was about an hour west of Detroit, but as we were already on our way there, we took them up on their gracious offer.

I was on cloud nine as we drove out of town, stopping at a desolate, bullet-riddled gas station to fill up the tank before the long drive, because that night I met another hardcore hero of mine, Laughing Hyenas lead singer John Brannon, who was once the singer of my favourite Detroit band, Negative Approach. I was living out my punk rock fantasy, not only meeting the people in my record collection but also sleeping on their fucking floors. The party began the moment we arrived, and soon everyone was drinking fiercely (among other things) while viewing Super 8 films on a little screen in the main area. Exhausted by the performance, I chose to leave early, preferring to sleep in the vehicle parked out front rather than toss and turn in this house of horrors. throughout the night

I awoke hours later with the van rolling along the highway. I sprang up from my sleeping bag, perplexed, and looked around, but everyone had gone, except for Pete, who was driving slowly, his face silhouetted with each passing streetlight. "Dude, where has everyone gone? "What are we doing?" As I wiped the sleep from my sluggish eyelids, I croaked. "Do you believe in miracles?" Pete asked, in his trademark Southern drawl. Hours earlier, as we were filling up our tank to begin our trek westward, Pete had left our "float bag" (a tiny bag containing all of the cash we had to our names, approximately $900) on top of the gas pump at that desolate, bullet-ridden gas station in one of the poorest neighbourhoods of town. When he realised it was gone, he rushed in the van and doubled back to Detroit at full speed in the unlikely possibility that it was still there. It was, miraculously, and we moved on. I began to realise that this whole affair may fall apart at any time. That suburban stability I had been conditioned to seek was now in the rearview mirror, and the thrill and mystery of this new independence fit me like a glove.

After a few performances, we'd crossed the Mississippi River, the furthest I'd ever been from home, and I was getting used to this new life of truck stops and toll booths. To truly see America, you must travel it mile by mile, as you will not only begin to comprehend the vastness of this magnificent country, but you will also notice how the climate and terrain change with each state boundary. TO BE TRULY APPRECIATED, THESE ARE THINGS THAT CANNOT BE LEARNED FROM AN OLD SCHOOLBOOK UNDER THE COLD CLASSROOM LIGHTS; THEY MUST BE SEEN, HEARD, AND FELT IN PERSON. Because I was discovering life firsthand, learning social and survival skills I still rely on to this day (e.g., knowing when to speak and when to shut the fuck up), the education I was receiving on the road proved far more valuable to me than any algebra or biology test I had ever failed. Though I was finally free to pursue my lifetime ambition, I still called my mother every now and then to reassure her that she had made the correct decision in letting me go. Even though we were hundreds of miles apart, I felt closer to her than anyone else and wanted her to know that the risk she had allowed me to take with my life was paying off. Cities like Kansas City, Boulder, and Salt Lake City rushed by as we made our way to the West Coast, leaving a path of beer cans and burned stages in our wake. Within a few weeks, we were driving through the Pacific Northwest's cold drizzle and towering evergreens, on our way to Tacoma's Community World Theater, where we would perform with a young band called Diddly Squat. Great name, but even better bassist, whom I would meet years later to join our own band. Yes, Foo Fighters bassist Nate Mendel was a teen punk like me, and our paths crossed a few times without official introduction, but that's how these things happen; you just have to let the world drive. It's a good thing it did.

It was finally time to travel to California, a place I never imagined seeing in my wildest dreams. It made as much sense to me to be standing in front of the Hollywood sign 2,670 miles away from my little lovely town as it did to plant a fucking flag on Pluto. Unfathomable. All I knew of America's most glamorised state was what I saw on television and in movies, so I imagined all the cops looking like they were in The Village People, all the kids looking like they were in The Bad News Bears, and all the women looking like Charlie's Angels. (It turns out I was correct.)

With only five days until the next event, we took our time driving out to Santa Cruz, a town I knew little about other than it was where Corey Haim's vampire masterpiece The Lost Boys was filmed. Years previously, Scream had been great friends with a Santa Cruz band named Bl'ast, and because almost everyone was in this underground network group, they were gracious enough to offer us a place to crash until our next gig, in San Francisco. The eight-hundred-mile drive was exhausting, but the scenery compensated for our claustrophobia. We travelled over the prehistoric Pacific Coast Ranges' mountain passes until we reached the Pacific Coast Highway, where we weaved between the towering redwoods while giant waves smashed along the cliffs. I was astounded. I considered this the payoff for having watched the landscape bloom into its natural beauty over long, laborious weeks and thousands of miles. I felt so fortunate, alive, and free.

As we came closer to town, Pete called ahead to our host, Bl'ast pal Steve Isles, and told him an estimated time of arrival. He returned to the van with fantastic news: Steve's mother, Sherri, was preparing a massive pasta dinner for us all, and we would be staying at their lovely A-frame house just down the street from the beach for the next four days. This was no longer a tour; it was Club Med. We rushed to our new digs after buying Sherri a bouquet of flowers and a bottle of wine at the grocery store, eager to escape the constraints of our van and feast like kings.

We were welcomed like family, and before long, mountains of pasta were being devoured and fat joints of the most incredible marijuana I'd ever seen were being passed around the table, the thick, delicious smoke rising in the air as we drank and recounted road stories. Sherri, to my surprise, was also smoking! This was California, after all. MY MOTHER struck me as cool. Sherri's generosity in taking in this motley crew of unkempt punk rockers, feeding us, smoking us out, and providing us with a warm place to sleep was nothing short of sainthood-level. It was the most unselfish display of hospitality I had ever witnessed. I passed off in my sleeping bag, my smile blurry and my tummy full.

Sherri was leaving town the next day, but she told us that the leftovers were in the fridge and the weed was in the cupboard. Jimmy and I exchanged glances and dashed to the cupboard, where we discovered a giant mason jar filled with the kind of cannabis you only see in a High Times centrefold. We took a hairy, fluorescent-green bud and rode down to the beach on two Vespa-style scooters we discovered in the garage, and there it was... the Pacific Ocean. As the sun fell on the horizon, I walked across the sand to the shore break and felt the freezing water wash over my feet. I'd made it. I HAD CROSSED THE COUNTRY ON NOTHING MORE THAN THE LOVE OF MUSIC AND THE WILL TO SURVIVE FROM ONE OCEAN TO THE OTHER.

It couldn't possibly be any better than this.

CHAPTER 3
SURE, I WANNA BE YOUR DOG!

Toronto, Ontario, Canada. June 22, 1990. A lovely afternoon in "the 6." Scream had just embarked on yet another North American tour in our faithful (but weird) Dodge van, beginning with a brief run of Canadian performances in two of my favourite cities on the planet, Montreal and Toronto. Scream had built a small but devoted fan base in the Great White North over the years, while also making friends with a network of incredible people who kindly hosted us in their various warehouse lofts and shared apartments whenever we came to visit (far more comfortable accommodations than we were used to at the time). I've always enjoyed visiting Canada since my first journey at the age of eighteen. The hash was tasty, the girls were cute, and the shows were always raucous, attracting enough paid entrants to get us to the next destination without too much trouble. But it was the unequalled hilarity of the post-show parties with our Canuck pals that made the trip worthwhile. Because, let's be honest, Canadians are fucking amazing. Laid-back, sincere, and hilarious as heck. I dare anyone to walk one city block in Canada without meeting a new friend. Our extended family of freaks and geeks always welcomed us with open arms, and they never failed to show us a good time, whether we were drunkenly wandering the streets of Montreal well past midnight in search of smoked-meat sandwiches and poutine, or getting high until the sun came up while watching Night Ride.

The Rivoli on Queen Street West was possibly the coolest club in town, out of all the venues in Toronto. With a capacity of roughly 250 people, it may not have been Royal Albert Hall, but it was perfectly suited to a band like ours, and we would definitely take the roof off the fuckin' building with a triple-digit decimal attack come showtime.During a pre-show soundcheck, I spotted the bartender plastering promotional posters for Iggy Pop's new album, Brick by Brick, all over the sticky, nicotine-stained walls. Strange, I thought, but since it had nothing to do with our performance, we all proceeded to plug in and turn up our high-octane punk rock and roll, getting our PA and monitor levels as close to perfect as we could for that night's performance. Our road crew consisted of one roadie at the time, Barry Thomas (very Canadian), thus the task of erecting our backline of equipment was primarily left to the band. There was no sound engineer or lighting designer, just the four of us and Barry. A club soundcheck was typically held in the late afternoon, just before doors opened, because set times were usually in the late evening. But, for whatever reason, we were instructed to arrive considerably earlier, at noon, for our 9 p.m. show on this specific day. That's unusual. Nonetheless, we did our best to comply. I had a sneaky sensation that something was up as I tuned my drums and saw more and more Iggy posters go up on the wall, so I stopped what I was doing and asked the bartender, "Hey, man, what's the deal with all the posters?"

"Iggy's having a record release party here before your show," he said casually. "And he's performing."

My brain nearly exploded. This was a joyful musical destiny miracle! What a coincidence to be in the right place at the right moment! I was about to enter the same dismal tiny room as punk's godfather, IGGY FUCKING POP! This man, once known as James Newell Osterberg Jr., was the Adam AND Eve of punk music, and he would soon transform this little hole-in-the-wall club into a sonic Garden of Eden! The phrase "living legend" does not begin to capture his significance and impact. I mean, he's the man who invented the fucking stage dive. That's not all!

"But you have to leave after soundcheck." It's solely for record labels."

My hopes of meeting this musical enigma were destroyed in an instant. I pleaded. I begged. I fought back the tears of a thousand Cure fans, racking my brain for any and every reason I could think of to persuade him that we should stay. "But, but... what about our gear?" We must be present to ensure that nothing is stolen!" I blurted out, hoping he'd accept the bait and let us off the hook. "The gear will be fine," he assured them. "It's just a bunch of record company types."

We finished our soundcheck, licking our wounds and cursing corporate, major-label album release parties to the flaming depths of hell, and fled back to our old rust bucket in the alley. We were heartbroken and rejected after being expelled from this once-in-a-lifetime experience, rivalled only by the time I was ditched at a senior homecoming dance (which was on a boat, so I was locked in adolescent purgatory until we docked hours later). If the term "FOMO" had existed in 1990, it would have surely applied here. Our two options were to roam the city in search of a drink or to wait in the vehicle for nine hours eating pizza and listening to the radio. I chose option B despite being rather hungover from the night before.

A black stretch limo emerged a short while later as we reclined in the van. It pulled into the back alley, stopped, and popped the trunk as the club door simultaneously swung open, a security guard awaiting the chauffeur's valuable cargo with the choreographed attention to detail that would be offered for a sitting president. We craned our necks in excitement as we peered out the window of our mobile homeless shelter to see our hero in person. And suddenly, just like in Daniel's vision of the angel, he appeared. He emerged from the automobile not far from our parking spot, all five feet and seven inches of rock royalty crammed into faded trousers and a T-shirt. He approached the trunk, grabbed his guitar case, and dashed inside. UP TO THIS POINT IN MY LIFE, I HAD NEVER BEEN THIS CLOSE TO A TRUE ROCK STAR. Years of studying his work had seared his gorgeous, crooked image into my mind, yet this was no one-dimensional album jacket or bedroom poster. In the flesh, this was the living, breathing personification of cool. And with that, the backstage door shut behind him.

I've waxed poetic before about the thrill of human interaction, particularly as it applies to live music, because it transports us from the one-dimensional virtual experience to the three-dimensional tangible experience, ultimately reassuring us that this life is real and that we are not alone. Even a random encounter with someone you've grown up listening to, staring at their album covers for hours on end, learning to play the drums by studying their jagged, tribal patterns, can flip the matrix. That was all I needed that night. My trust in music was strengthened simply by watching Iggy go the short distance from his automobile into the same dark door I had just exited. My world has become a little brighter. That was the end of it.

I followed along as best I could, having never heard the music before, but I couldn't help but wonder why he was bothering to teach me something that no one would ever hear. Maybe he was just bored and wanted to jam? Maybe he was graciously fulfilling some no-name kid's dream by encouraging me to play along with him, knowing it was a story I'd get to tell for the rest of my life? As weird as it was, I kept my attention on his strumming hand and locked into the arrangement, bashing it out like we were in a sold-out stadium. We ended in synchrony with a joyful last crash.

"Great," he exclaimed after we were finished. "We go on at six o'clock."

Wait, what? Us? This? Tonight? This was not at all what I expected. I never imagined he'd want to sing these songs with me IN FRONT OF PEOPLE. I assumed it was just an impromptu jam session, something I'd done a thousand times before with pals in basements and dusty garages packed with gasoline cans and gardening tools to pass the time. I had no idea this was an audition! "You wanna do this tonight?" I asked, my jaw dropping. "Yeah, man!" said Iggy. "Ummmm . . . should we have a bass player?" I enquired. "You got one?" he asked, startled. I dashed out to the van to get our bassist, Skeeter. I couldn't wait to share this life-changing experience with another bandmate, knowing he'd appreciate it just as much as I did. Skeeter was a major fan of Iggy and the Stooges (not to mention a phenomenal bass player with perfect time and feel), and the three of us were prepared and ready in no time. It was official: we were now Iggy Pop's rhythm section, at least for one night in Toronto.

We hung out with Iggy in the tiny dressing area offstage when the record label arrived, smoking cigarettes and listening to anecdotes from his legendary career. THIS MADMAN, REVERED FOR LIVE PERFORMANCES IN WHICH HE SMEARED PEANUT BUTTER ALL OVER HIS BODY, CUT HIMSELF WITH SHARDS OF GLASS, AND EXPOSED HIMSELF TO THE AUDIENCE, WAS NOTHING BUT A FRIENDLY, WARM, DOWN-TO-EARTH GENTLEMAN. As if things couldn't get any crazier! He made us feel completely at ease, and our nerves quickly evolved to excited anticipation. Every now and then, there would be a tap on the door, and a label representative would ask, "Need anything?" Skeeter and I quickly discovered that these people assumed we were Iggy's band! So, without hesitation, we began to explore how much we could milk this already inconceivable sensation. "A pack of smokes?" Done. "A case of beer?" No issue. "A carton of smokes?" Absolutely. Then it hit me: This is how it feels to make it. No more sleeping in a chilly van with four other guys, crammed like sardines in sleeping bags on a plywood platform, rationing $7.50 per day on Taco Bell and lousy pot. No more returning home and asking for my work back after each tour, patiently waiting for the next to whisk me away from my high-school dropout reality. There will be no waiting in strewn alleyways for your chance at a fictitious celebrity. I knew that this sense of accomplishment would pass quickly, so I took a mouthful instead of just a taste.

We took the stage to Iggy Pop-sized applause. "FUUUUCK YOU!!!" he screamed over the microphone as we counted into the first song, "1969," and the audience erupted. He was no longer the kind, down-to-earth gentleman I had just met backstage; instead, he was suddenly transformed into the Iggy punk fans all over the world know and love. Tearing through song after song, I barely had time to ponder on the full-circle aspect of this fantastic twist of fate, so I surrendered to the moment and banged the living shit out of that gigantic yellow drum set like it was my last night on earth. Every now and again, I'd peek up through my filthy hair to see his chiselled, crooked frame stalking the stage, just like in all of those legendary one-dimensional photographs and films I'd seen a thousand times before. Except now he was three-dimensional, reminding me that life is real and that I am not alone. It was over in a matter of minutes, far too quickly, and with complimentary cigarettes and beer in hand, we thanked Iggy and parted ways. I'D FINALLY MADE IT," EVEN IF ONLY FOR ONE NIGHT, AND IT WAS EXACTLY HOW I'D ALWAYS DREAMED IT WOULD BE. It's too wonderful to be true. So, without being disappointed, I appreciated it for the lovely experience that it was. Expecting to be at the right place at the right time again was almost impossible. What were the odds?

Our Scream trip continued, albeit not without complications. The Midwest performances that were supposed to get us to the West Coast were cancelled, so we had to drive the four thousand miles to Olympia, Washington, with nothing but those complimentary cigarettes and the money in our pockets. With nothing to lose, we decided to go for it. After all, we'd come this far; what was another long trek across America?

We had no idea it would be our final.

CHAPTER 4
EVERY DAY IS A BLANK PAGE

"Anyone seen Skeeter?"

We began to emerge from our sleeping bags on the crowded living room floor of the old Hollywood bungalow that we had been sharing with a few Hollywood Tropicana mud wrestlers, a little hungover from another wild night in Laurel Canyon, and took a head count. Check, Pete. Check, Franz. Check, Barry. Skeeter, on the other hand, was nowhere to be found. I closed my eyes and crossed my fingers that, first and foremost, Skeeter was okay, but also that he hadn't left us stranded on tour thousands of miles from home with no money and no way back. Given that he'd previously disappeared, this was a genuine fear.

By 1990, my travels with Scream had taken me from Louisiana to Ljubljana, Memphis to Milan, San Francisco to Stockholm, and I had become a seasoned road warrior, no stranger to the occasional crisis or conflict, so having one member missing in action was just another day on the road. What had once been a crash course in how to exist on less than $10 per day in a van had become a familiar, comfortable routine, and I had readily integrated into the life of a roving vagrant. The European travels were especially fascinating since we visited countries I had only seen on the evening news or read about in my horribly neglected textbooks. Instead of the normal historic tourist sites that most people visit when going abroad, I was discovering the globe through the sordid underbelly of the underground punk rock scene. Since Scream had previously toured Europe before I joined the band, they had already formed a network that welcomed us as family, providing us with places to stay, food to eat, and equipment to use on tour because we couldn't afford to transport our own instruments from home. Most of those pals were musicians as well, and the majority of them lived in squats, abandoned buildings teeming with punks and anarchists, frequently stealing utilities from the city grid to exist. These radical communities were not only intriguing to my young, impressionable mind, but also inspiring, because life in these makeshift communes was stripped down to the most basic human elements, foregoing the trappings of conventional existence (materialism, greed, and social status) in favour of a life of protest, freedom, and the realisation that we all need each other to get by. I thought it was all rather lovely, a far cry from the suburban white-picket-fence mindset I had left behind at home. The simple exchange of a warm bed for a song laid the groundwork for my appreciation of becoming a musician, which I still use to get perspective when I feel lost in the tsunami of my now much more complicated life.

Amsterdam had become our home base for a variety of reasons, some obvious (marijuana), others purely logistical (proximity to Northern Europe). We'd usually save up our money from our menial day jobs at home and fly standby on a Dutch airline called Martinair for $99, arrive at Schiphol international airport, steal a bike the first night, and spend the next few weeks preparing for our tour by making phone calls with a pirated phone card, gathering gear, and renting a van that would become our home for the next few months. To make ends meet, we would return bottles at the night shop, try our luck at the gaming machines in the taverns, and even accept odd jobs here and there. (I used to work at Konkurrent, a little mail-order record company, cramming boxes full of CDs to be mailed all over the world to fund my cannabis habit until the tour started.) It was basic, but the hospitality and camaraderie shown to us by our gracious friends made us feel like we were living in opulence, and I eventually fell in love with the city so much that I attempted to learn Dutch, a language I'm convinced is impossible to speak if you weren't born in Holland.

BUT, MORE THAN ANYTHING, I WAS FREE, AND ADVENTURE WAS RIGHT AROUND THE CORNER.

When we were all drinking on the pavement in front of our favourite punk rock bar, De Muur, one night in Amsterdam, there was a sudden explosion of activity across the street at the Vrankrijk, one of Holland's most famed squats. An army of skinheads and right-wing fascists had planned an attack on the building, and as they marched up the short street, the Vrankrijk residents braced themselves for fight. As punks began pouring out of the squat with handmade weapons and shields, blinding flood lights turned on from the balconies and chicken wire fell down over the windows. A full-fledged riot erupted, and before long we were all joining in, tossing our glasses of beer into the air and raining them down on the mob of enraged fascists in shattered glass bursts like catapults releasing warm malted bombs. Within minutes, the intruders surrendered and fled, and we went about our business, now celebrating the uprising like Vikings returning from war. This wasn't exactly rock and roll. This was mediaeval nonsense. And that was only a Tuesday night.

Travelling across Europe's beautiful countryside became my favourite hobby, perhaps more so than driving down the lengthy, monotonous superhighways of our American travels, but it came with its own set of obstacles. We were exposed to a different language every week as we moved from country to country, and communication was reduced to a primitive kind of sign language that bordered on comical miming. Having said that, I was learning about languages and cultures that I would not have learned in school, and the physicality of being in these places improved my sense of the world as a community, which is much smaller than most people imagine. But the border crossings were always entertaining... picture a customs official's delight when a gang of young punks pulled up in a van with Netherlands licence plates (large red flag) with guitars and amps (bigger red flag). They would line us up like convicts on the pavement and tear our vehicle to tears seeking for any and all contraband, like shooting fish in a barrel. (I must admit that I've had more than a few body cavity searches over the years.) Having seen the 1978 film Midnight Express one too many times, we were all responsible enough to know that we should all smoke up all our pot or hash before crossing any border, for fear of rotting away in a dark, damp prison. Having said that, there was always a way to avoid "the man." Whether it was stuffing our speaker cabinets full of Scream T-shirts to sell at shows (our bread and butter on the road) to avoid taxation from country to country or hiding small chunks of hash in Skeeter's dreadlocks so we'd all have something to smoke on the long drives between shows (there's nothing like watching our bassist play with the drug dog at the border, knowing full well that his tangled mop was filled with ounces of spicy black hash), But not without a few near misses along the way. When I was going down an Amsterdam alleyway with my old friend Marco Pisa, an Italian tattoo artist I met in Bologna when I painted his tattoo shop in exchange for a beautiful branding on my left shoulder, we were approached by two junkies trying to sell us heroin. We weren't fans of heroin (or junkies), so Marco respectfully declined with a firm "Fuck off!" and we continued walking. They persisted, closely following us and tapping our shoulders, until Marco took out a switchblade with ninja speed and yelled, "FUCK OFF!" Stunned, I turned to walk away when I observed one of the junkies poised to bash me in the head with a metal pipe he had picked up from a work site we were passing. Marco and I raced off like a shot, pursued by a horde of shrieking zombies, just outrunning them before enjoying a lovely Thai lunch by the picturesque canals.

It was enough to make anyone want to pack their belongings and fly home to the comfort of their warm bed, but it was the sense of danger that kept me from doing so. EVERY DAY WAS A BLANK PAGE WAITING TO BE WRITE, FROM DODGY RENTAL VEHICLES DRIVING THROUGH APOCALYPTIC SCANDINAVIAN SNOWSTORMS AT NIGHT, TO PASSPORTS BEING STOLEN FROM YOUR ROOM AS YOU SLEPT, TO FISTFIGHTS WITH DRUNKEN ASSHOLES TRYING TO STEAL GEAR OR SWAG FROM THE VAN.

Even in the depths of my anguish and starvation, I never considered capitulation. What did I have to return to? pleading with my supervisor at the furniture warehouse to let me return to ten-hour days of painting gaudy sleeping sofas with dangerous 3M chemicals? A lifetime of suffocating rush-hour traffic, with strip malls and fast-food joints on every corner? I'd rather have been delirious in a tiny Spanish apartment, shivering in a pool of my own sweat from a horrible flu as the bustling Las Ramblas neighbourhood of Barcelona echoed below. I'd rather have slept on a freezing nightclub stage in Linköping, Sweden, after the event while paramedics rushed in to save a drug overdose victim. I'd rather have been advised not to eat the pasta served by a local promoter who was attempting to poison us in retaliation for a broken toilet than have driven up to play a squat in Italy where they were burning their linens outside after a scabies outbreak. As the saying goes, "ride or die." But it's possible that Skeeter abandoned us the first time because of our unstable lifestyle. In the spring of 1990, during what would be my final European tour with Scream, he decided that he just couldn't hang and flew home, leaving us stranded on another continent thousands of miles away. We were fortunate to have our dear buddy Guy Pinhas fill in for a few performances, allowing us to continue the tour with just enough money to catch the standby flights back on El Al airlines, but I was beginning to suspect that Skeeter's dedication to the band was not the same as Pete's, Franz's, and mine. We would have done anything to prevent the wheels from falling off.

Though none of us were irreplaceable, the chemistry between the four of us was undeniable, and Skeeter and I had a certain groove together, which he had instilled in me years before during one of our early rehearsals, and which was sorely missed when we played with a substitute bassist. When I initially joined Scream, I was like a wild pony, playing as fast and as hard as I could, slapping meaningless drum fills at the end of every phrase to dazzle anyone within earshot. Skeeter sat me down one day, rolled a massive joint from the paper wrapper of a tampon discovered in the bathroom, and got me so high I couldn't see straight. "Okay, we're gonna play one riff, the same riff, for thirty minutes and you're not going to do one drumroll," he told me. Simple, I reasoned. I sat behind my kit as he started playing his silky bass line, half reggae, part Motown, and I boldly joined in. It didn't take me 45 seconds to feel the temptation to do a drumroll, but he shook his head and advised me not to, so I kept going with the beat. A minute later, I had the unquenchable want to do a crazy drumroll, almost like a musical Tourette's or hold back a sneeze, but Skeeter merely shook his head. Skeeter was essentially breaking the wild pony, teaching me to respect the simplicity and strength of a rhythm and to stop from unnecessary bluster. I was a completely different drummer after thirty minutes. This was possibly the most important musical instruction I've ever received, and I'll be eternally grateful to him for it.

The few replacements who filled his shoes on subsequent trips were excellent musicians, but when Skeeter asked to return, we couldn't say no, even though we were afraid he'd disappear again. Things appeared to be looking bright for the band at the moment, as we had recently recorded a fresh set of songs that piqued the interest of a fellow punk rocker turned music industry insider, who offered to help us find a spot for it at a much bigger label. A friend of a friend and a man of tremendous integrity in the punk rock world, he offered us a contract to sign that would allow him to shop our tape around and find us a deal. This could be it, we reasoned. Perhaps this was our ticket out of the streets teeming with junkies and scabies-infested squatters to which we had become accustomed over the years. As tempting as it was to sign it right away, we decided to give it some thought before entrusting our life to a complete stranger.

We didn't pull out the contract and read it in the back of our van until one blazing hot day in Spokane months later, sitting in the parking lot of a Denny's after many performances across the country had been cancelled. Because we didn't at this point. The walls were closing in on us, and no matter how hard we tried, it never seemed to be enough. We signed that contract out of desperation, without any legal assistance, in a dangerous act of naiveté. One that would come back to bother me a year later, when that "punk rock man of great integrity" sued me, a twenty-one-year-old child, for joining Nirvana, thus claiming ownership. This was my debut to the music industry, ladies and gentlemen. At the very least, there was Los Angeles to look forward to.

Los Angeles was always the highlight of every tour, not just for the obvious benefits of a few days in hairspray heaven, but also because we had relatives there: Pete and Franz's sister, Sabrina. Sabrina was the most fun, bubbliest, most gorgeous lady you'd ever seen, having moved from the dull suburbs of Virginia to the glitter of Los Angeles in the late 1980s. We would stay at her apartment whenever we were in town, and she would take us about like an eighties video vixen chaperone, from the brilliant lights of the Sunset Strip to her place of business, the Hollywood Tropicana. Sabrina used to be a mud wrestler. For those unfamiliar, it is the act of two individuals wrestling in a pit of "mud," which may or may not be genuine mud but something that resembles Silly String and frying oil (don't ask me, I've never had the pleasure). It is a very casual affair, usually consisting of one woman in a bikini versus a drunken businessman who blew the majority of his entertainment budget on the company card to have his ass handed to him by a five-foot-eleven supermodel in a neon swimsuit. I mean, these ladies happily beat the living shit out of these boys, leaving most of them to be taken away with ruptured genitals crying in agony while the spectators roared with the ferocity of Romans in the Colosseum. As tough as it was for Pete and

Franz to see their younger sister jump into a muddy pit with a complete stranger, we would all go down for free drinks and collapse in spasms of laughter as each victim was hauled away one by one. And after the ruthless carnage, we'd return to Sabrina's Laurel Canyon bungalow, which she shared with a few other mud wrestlers, and party all night. The word "slumming" does not spring to mind.

Los Angeles interested me almost as much as Europe's millennia of history, but in a far different way. Everything appeared to be... incredible. As much as Washington, DC, could be described as a transitory city, with its social dynamic moving radically with each new government, Los Angeles seemed to change by the minute. People came and went via a revolving door of opportunity and demise, leaving their filth behind for the next wave of visitors to wade through in the goal of becoming the next big thing, as if it were the world's largest Greyhound bus station. There was a sadness that seemed to be covered by excess and overindulgence, making the hangovers that much more difficult to drink away the next morning. Nothing could be more depressing than waking up in a sleeping bag on a mud wrestler's floor, hoping your band member didn't abandon you high and dry. Again. We had to call and cancel the gig we had booked for that night because there was no sign of Skeeter by six p.m. Reality began to set in. Skeeter's absence meant no show. There would be no money if there was no show. Without money, there was no food. And no tour meant no ticket home, leaving me with the terrifying prospect of spending the rest of my life amid the desolate desperation of America's most glamorous city, wallowing through filth as its newest victim. We'd dug our way out of a lot of holes over the years, but this one seemed especially deep.

The days passed, and we managed to subsist as strays thanks to the generosity of our mud-wrestling housemates, who returned home every night emptying their purses full of dollar bills into enormous piles on the living room carpet. Food was sparse, and hunger set in quickly. Our roadie, Barry the Canadian, was receiving Social Security payments to assist keep us from going hungry, but they only lasted so long. To this day, I will never say "doesn't amount to a can of beans," because I recall finding a can of beans in that kitchen one day and it literally saved my fucking life. The going was challenging, but having been conditioned to survive any obstacle by years on the road, I did my best to keep my head up. It was not an easy task. I ultimately obtained a job tiling a coffee shop in Costa Mesa to supplement my income, but as time passed, it became clear that we weren't going anywhere anytime soon. Understandably, Barry returned to Canada after understanding that our condition was hopeless. I was beginning to despair and needed even a sliver of relief or rescue from our slowly sinking ship. Our stuff was collecting dust in Sabrina's downstairs garage, but after a week or so, I saw something else collecting dust in that small garage: a black 1985 Honda Rebel 250 cc motorcycle. It was a lovely little motorcycle, like a Fisher-Price version of a Harley-Davidson, only one step above a moped but ideal for darting around town. I raced upstairs and questioned who owned this glamorised minibike, having always fantasised of owning a motorcycle (literally a recurring dream throughout my life). It turned out to be the property of one of Sabrina's mud-wrestling housemates, who said, "Sure, take it! Simply fill it up with gas and it's yours!"

MY LIFEBOAT WAS REDUCED.

I waited for the sun to go down, filled the Rebel's tiny tank with gas, and took off through the hills, avoiding any major thoroughfares for fear of being pulled over and, well... because I didn't know how to ride a fucking motorcycle. I left all of my problems on the floor of Sabrina's cluttered living room and drove aimlessly through the winding maze of the affluent Hollywood Hills, looking down at the shimmering lights of the city below and up at the countless gorgeous houses nestled in the trees, dreaming of one day living in such luxury. Each one was no doubt occupied by a rock star, a movie star, a producer or director who had followed their dreams and somehow struck gold, and I wondered how it must feel to achieve that level of success, to live in such comfort, and to know where your next meal was coming from. The gap between this ideal and my reality was so vast, so unfathomable, that it wasn't even worth contemplating. So I simply drove. This was my way out. This was my momentary salvation. This was my lifeboat from the sinking ship in the distance. And while I raced through the night, I reflected on everything that had taken me here, retracing my steps while attempting to plan the next. I followed this cycle night after night, waking up in my sleeping bag on the living room floor with my eyes virtually swollen shut from the dust and grit of the canyon roads, returning to the reality of being a mud wrestler's stray pet. THEN I HEARD THE FIVE WORDS THAT FOREVER CHANGED MY LIFE: "HAVE YOU HEARD OF NIRVANA?"

On a phone contact with an old friend who had grown up in Aberdeen, Washington, with the Nirvana guys, I learned that they were in between drummers at the time and had seen Scream perform just weeks earlier on our ill-fated tour. They were apparently impressed with my performance, and I was given their phone numbers to call. Of course, I was familiar with Nirvana. Bleach, their debut album, was a milestone record in the underground music scene, fusing metal, punk, and Beatles-esque melody into an eleven-song masterpiece that would go on to revolutionise the landscape of "alternative" music (while also costing $606). It rapidly became one of my favourites and stuck out from the rest of my noisy, heavy punk records because it had SONGS. And that voice... no one else has a voice like it...

After a few more days of frustration and famine, I decided to take a chance and phone Nirvana's bassist, Krist, to inquire about the drummer position. I introduced myself and said that a common acquaintance had given me his number, so we talked for a bit until Krist informed me that the post of drummer had already been taken by their good buddy Dan Peters from Mudhoney. It was worth a shot, I reasoned, but it wasn't the end of the world. I gave Krist my Los Angeles phone number and told him to remain in touch and give me a call if they ever came down to L.A., because it was starting to look like the City of Angels was unfortunately now my permanent domicile.

The house phone rang the same night. Krist returned my call. He appears to have given the topic considerable thought. "Maybe you should talk to Kurt," he said. Danny Peters, while an incredible drummer in his own right, had a totally different approach than mine, playing with a more sixties rudimental feel as opposed to my basic, Neanderthal disco dynamic, which felt more Nirvana-esque. Furthermore, Krist and Kurt felt a little awful plucking Danny from Mudhoney, one of their all-time favourite bands. So I called Kurt right away and we spoke about music for a long time. We discovered that we had a lot in common musically, from NWA to Neil Young, Black Flag to the Beatles, the Cramps to Creedence Clearwater Revival, and that an audition could be worth pursuing. "Well, if you can make it up here, just let us know," he replied casually in his now-famous drawl. We said our goodbyes, and I was now left with one of the most difficult decisions of my life.

I'd felt like a part of a family since the day I joined Scream. Despite my age, Pete, Franz, and Skeeter always regarded me as an equal, and we became close friends, spending practically every day together, tour or no tour. I had spent the most formative years of my life with them, discovering music, discovering the world, and ultimately discovering myself, so moving on and leaving them behind in that sinking ship broke my heart in ways I had never felt before, even more than saying goodbye to my own father when he disowned me for dropping out of high school. We'd always been in this together, all for one and one for all, and we'd been through so much crap. But there was something final about this new dilemma that made me wonder about my future. So, anytime I had doubts about my future, whenever I needed a voice of reason or some words of wisdom, I phoned the one person who had never once led me astray... my mother.

On a collect call from the parking lot of an Orange County record store, I sadly recounted my predicament, and she completely understood since she felt the same way about Pete and Franz as I did. We'd all become a family over the years, and she saw them as more than just my bandmates; they were my brothers. I'll never forget the sound of her voice offering me the guidance that turned my life in the right direction.

"David... I know you care about your friends, but sometimes you have to prioritise your own needs over those of others." You must look for yourself." This came from a woman whose entire life had been the polar opposite of that, but because she was the wisest person I knew, I hung up the phone and vowed to follow her advice regardless of the consequences.

I put my duffel bag, sleeping bag, and drum kit into a cardboard moving box and drove up to Seattle, a city I had only visited once and where I knew almost no one, to begin a new life. I felt a sense of loss that I had never felt before. I was homesick. I was missing my friends. I was missing my family. I was now genuinely on my own, starting from scratch. However, I was still hungry. And, because I'm not one to let my wheels spin, I had to keep going. After all, I was still free, and adventure awaited around every corner.

I still drive by that old house, that sinking ship in Laurel Canyon, virtually every day, and it has slowly crumbled under its own weight over the years, slipping beneath the surface in time. But the memories and lessons I acquired during that time have stayed with me, and I now take my own lifeboat for a nightly sail whenever I need to take stock and retrace my steps while planning the next.

BECAUSE EVERY DAY IS STILL A BLANK PAGE DYING TO BE WRITE.

CHAPTER 5
IT'S A FOREVER THING

"Would you mind if we took a break?" "I've never had a tribal tattoo done before."

Believe me, these are not the words you want to hear from a man as he drills a needle full of black ink into your flesh a thousand times per second as you desperately attempt to bear the blistering anguish of being forever branded without crying like a baby. But the beads of sweat streaming down his brow and his squinting red eyes were clearly not a good omen, so I got up from my chair and stepped outside for a quick smoke, wiping my brow with a paper towel. The complicated pattern I had created (based on the original John Bonham "three circles" emblem) had to be razor sharp, with straight, even lines and flawless circles interlaced to create a piece that would wrap around my right wrist like a threatening Celtic bracelet. Even for a seasoned professional, this was no simple assignment, and his tired irritation was far from encouraging. Nonetheless, it had to be correct, and there was no turning back now. AFTER ALL, IT'S A PERMANENT THING.

It was the fall of 1990 in Olympia, Washington, and I had just received my first check from Nirvana as a paid member. It was by far the greatest payout of my professional life up until that point, a whooping $400. This much-needed advance from our newly acquired management business, Gold Mountain, arrived at a time when Nirvana was being courted by every major-label record company known to man in an all-out bidding war, while Kurt and I were physically hungry and living in squalor. Our 114 NE Pear Street apartment was the back unit of a decaying old home built around 1914, with one bedroom, one bathroom, a small living room, and a kitchen the size of a broom closet (ironically located directly across the street from the Washington State lottery facility). It was not Versailles. The word "unclean" doesn't even begin to convey the carnage inside. It transformed the Chelsea Hotel into a Four Seasons. Whitney Houston's restroom has been turned inside out. The aftermath of a trailer-park tornado of ashtrays and magazines. Most people would never enter such a dangerous cave, but that was our humble shelter, and we considered it home. Kurt slept in the bedroom, while I slept in my sleeping bag on an old brown couch covered in cigarette burns and falling far short of my six-foot frame. Kurt had a pet turtle in a horrible terrarium at the end of the couch on an old table. Kurt, a true animal lover, had an odd, possibly metaphorical fondness for turtles, whose shells, the item that best protected them, were actually incredibly sensitive. "Like having your spine on the outside of your body," he once remarked. But, as lovely and anatomically poetic as that feeling was, it didn't matter since this goddamned reptile kept me awake every night, tapping its head against the glass for hours on end in an attempt to escape our shared home of filth. I couldn't hold it against the poor thing. I frequently felt the same way.

At the time, I was surviving on a three-for-ninety-nine-cent corn dog special from the Ampm petrol station across the street. The trick was to eat one for breakfast (at noon) and save the other two for a late dinner after rehearsal, which kept me going until hunger pangs set in and I was forced to return to the fluorescent glow of the convenience store lights with another crumpled dollar bill in my hand. (I still tremble when I see a battered frank skewered on a jagged wooden stick.) It was just enough to keep my twenty-one-year-old metabolism humming, but it provided no meaningful nutritional benefit. This impoverished diet, along with my penchant for playing the drums with every fibre of my thin being five evenings a week, had reduced me to a virtual waiflike marionette, barely filling out the soiled old clothes I kept in a duffel bag on the floor in the corner of the living room. It was enough to send anyone running back to the comforts of their mother's home cooking, but I was 2,786 miles away in Springfield, Virginia. And then I was free.

On the Faces' legendary 1973 song "Ooh La La," Ronnie Wood sang, "I wish I knew what I know now when I was younger." Oh, Ronnie... if only you knew. Truer words were never spoken. This $400 advance was by far the most money I had ever seen in my life! In my head, I was suddenly Warren Buffett! As the son of a Fairfax County public school teacher, my childhood was anything from frivolous, and I learned to live well within my means, working as hard as I could to make ends meet while finding delight in the little things in life. Music, friends, and family are all important to me. I'd never made so much money mowing lawns, painting houses, preparing furniture for delivery trucks, or working the cash register at Tower Records in downtown Washington, DC. This was a big moment, as far as I was concerned. I had finally hit the lottery, but instead of saving and budgeting this large sum to assure survival (think the mountains of corn dogs!), I did what most new musicians do with their first check: I squandered it on crap.

In retrospect, I now see why I went straight to Fred Meyer to get a BB pistol and a Nintendo console. Clearly, I was indulging in childhood luxuries that I had wished for but never received when I was younger. Not to say I was a happy or deprived youngster, but any extra money in my family was kept for more practical things like new shoes or winter jackets (there was once a fifty-dollar minibike, but that's another story). My diligent mother worked numerous jobs to make ends meet: school teacher by day, department store clerk by night, and weekend estimate writer for Servpro, a carpet cleaning firm. She did everything she could as a single mother with two young children to keep us happy and healthy. We certainly were. She raised me to be a true altruist in every meaning of the term, to need very little and to give very lot. Her work ethic is strongly ingrained in me, and I owe her a debt of gratitude for where I am today. The nagging feeling that I need to be productive that keeps me awake at night and wakes me up in the morning can be directly traced back to the long nights she would spend grading papers at the living room desk under an old lamp, only to wake up before the sun to make sure my sister and I walked out the front door bathed, dressed, and fed. Granted, my job is insignificant in comparison to her career as an educator, but she has taught me the value of perseverance. So, $400 for a night of loud, dissonant rock and roll? Money for nothing!

Soon, our afternoons in Olympia were spent shooting egg cartons from a distance in our old house's backyard and playing Super Mario World till the sun came up (we may or may not have taken a few potshots at the lottery building across the street in the cause of the revolution). Our filthy den had been turned into an adolescent leisure centre from hell. This was Versailles to me. However, because I had neither foresight or care for realistic spending, the money quickly ran out, leaving me with just enough money for one more crazy indulgence: a tattoo. Not my first, to be sure. No, that was a self-inflicted masterpiece I created at the age of fourteen with a sewing needle, some thread, and a jug of black ink. After viewing Uli Edel's gritty homemade-tattoo scene in Christiane F., I decided to bedazzle my left forearm in the same DIY method with the insignia of my favourite band at the time, Black Flag. I waited until everyone was asleep, set up a temporary tattoo studio in my bedroom, and began my evil operation after gathering all of the necessary components from the dusty garbage drawers around the house. I sterilised the sewing needle with candle fire, gently wrapped the tiny thread around the tip, and dipped it into the jar of ink, seeing the fibres soak up the thick black liquid, just like in the movie. Then I began with a steady hand. Poke, poke, poke, poke, poke. The sting of the needle as it entered my skin sent chills down my spine, and I paused every now and then to wipe away the surplus of clouded pigment and assess the damage. I wasn't Kat Von D, but I persisted, inserting the needle as deeply as my pain level would allow to ensure that this profound image would never disappear. If you've seen the classic Black Flag emblem, you'll recognize it as four thick, black vertical bars in staggered sequence. A tall order for a run-down youngster with his mother's seldom-used sewing kit. I made it through three of the four bars before saying, "Fuuuuck this shit!" and stopping. Not the show-stopping moment I had hoped for, but my heart was suddenly filled with a sense of finality that strangely emboldened me. Something that will last forever.

I accumulated quite a collection of these little blurred diaries all over my body over the years. A little mark here, a little mark there, until I was ultimately graced with the opportunity to get legitimately tattooed by Andrea Ganora, an Italian artist who lived in the famed Amsterdam squat Van Hall. The facility, an old two-story factory, had been taken over and occupied by a small group of punk rockers from all over Europe in late 1987. The frigid, enormous structure was converted into their home by a tight-knit community of friends, complete with a live music club downstairs (where I accidentally made my first live record, SCREAM Live! at Van Hall, in 1988). It became a virtual home base for Scream when I was eighteen. Andrea was the resident tattoo artist, and the majority of Van Hall's residents proudly displayed his work. He was a true artist, but unlike most sanctioned tattoo establishments, his studio was his bedroom, and his tattoo gun was fashioned from an old doorbell machine. As our laughter and the electrifying buzz of his tattoo gun filled the room, we smoked joint after joint and listened to punk and metal albums. I can still recall the pleasure of my first "real" tattoo and am reminded of his strong Italian accent and the wonderful smell of hash every time I look in the mirror at the present he bestowed to me that night. Its hue hasn't faded even after 33 years.

My honeymoon on Pear Street soon ended, and I was back to rationing corn dogs and cursing the relentless tapping of the turtle terrarium night after night, head buried in the soiled cushions of that old couch. The lesson has been learned. The season grew dark, and homesickness struck in. I'd left my friends, family, and Virginia behind for... this. The harsh Pacific Northwest winter weather and lack of sunlight just exacerbated the growing sense of sadness, but happily, I still had one thing keeping me from retiring back home: the music. Even though Nirvana may be dysfunctional at times, there was an underlying focus whenever we put our instruments on and the amps started to shine. WE WANTED TO BE THE BEST. Alternatively, as Kurt once told music entrepreneur and giant Donnie Ienner in his New York City high-rise office, "We want to be the biggest band in the world." (I assumed he was joking.) Our rehearsal facility was a barn-like structure converted into a demo studio thirty minutes north of Olympia in a Tacoma suburb. It was one little step above an old, wet cellar, had heat and a modest PA system (not to mention some iffy shag carpeting), and serviced our basic needs admirably. Kurt and I would eagerly make the trip five days a week in a Datsun B210 handed to him by an elderly lady, barely making it up Interstate 5 without the wheels falling apart (one did once, lug nuts scattering across the gravel road in the dark). Our music was the one thing that kept my mind off the flaws of this new life I'd found, the only thing that made it all worthwhile. Every rehearsal began with a "noise jam," which evolved into an improvisational exercise in dynamics, eventually honing our collective instinct and allowing song structure to happen without needing to be verbally arranged; it would just happen, almost like a flock of blackbirds gracefully ebbs and flows in a hypnotic wave over a country field in the winter. Despite the fact that we did not originate it, this strategy was critical to the quiet/loud dynamic for which we became known. That was owing to our heroes, the Pixies, who had a major influence on us. We'd embraced their simple signature in several of our new songs: tight, concise verses that explode into massive, screaming choruses. A sonic clash that produces fierce results, most notably "Smells Like Teen Spirit."

As the long winter gave way to spring, we spent many hours in that makeshift studio working on songs for the album that would become Nevermind. Unlike the other bands I had been in, Nirvana did not play shows frequently for fear of exhausting the local audience, so the majority of our attention was focused on being ready to record once we had decided on a label and producer. Kurt was a wonderfully prolific songwriter, seemingly having a new song idea almost every week, so there was always a sense of forward motion, never feeling trapped or stagnant musically. After he shut his bedroom door at night, I would hear the peaceful strumming of a guitar from his room and wait for his light to go out from the comfort of my filthy old couch. Every day, I couldn't wait to hear whether he'd come up with something new once we got to rehearsal and plugged in. Whether it was music or entries in his now-famous notebooks, his drive to create was astounding, albeit he kept it almost entirely to himself. His tunes would sneak up on you and catch you off guard. And they were never preceded with the words "Hey, I wrote something great!" They would simply... emerge.

When I joined Nirvana in September 1990, the band had already finished recording a new batch of songs with their previous drummer, Chad Channing, for their next Sub Pop release. Butch Vig, a young up-and-coming producer from Madison, Wisconsin, had recorded songs like "In Bloom," "Imodium" (which became "Breed"), "Lithium," and "Polly" earlier that year. These songs had outgrown the previous material and promised great things to come, showcasing Kurt's ever-evolving songwriting ability. Simply put, Nirvana was evolving. This recording, combined with Butch's mega-fucking-rock sound, was responsible for the majority of the industry "buzz" surrounding the band, eventually igniting an ensuing feeding frenzy of interest. Most bands would have been embarrassed by these songs, but Kurt kept writing, and the new songs kept coming. "Come As You Are," "Drain You," "On a Plain," "Territorial Pissings," and then there's "Smells Like Teen Spirit." Usually starting with a Kurt riff, Krist Novoselic and I would follow his lead with our practised intuition, serving as the engine room to his screaming vision. My job was simple! I could always tell when a chorus was coming by watching Kurt's dirty Converse sneaker move closer and closer to the distortion pedal, and just before he stomped on the button, I'd blast into a single-stroke snare roll with all of my might, signalling the change. The ensuing eruption would frequently send chills up my spine, as the undeniable power of our collective sound had grown almost too large for that tiny little space. THESE SONGS WOULD NOT LAST LONG. They would soon surprise everyone by sneaking up on them.

It was a no-brainer for me to sign with the David Geffen Company. Following in the footsteps of legendary New York noise heroes Sonic Youth, we hired their manager, John Silva, and believed that any major-label record company brave enough to endorse Sonic Youth's experimental brand of no wave was a safe haven for a band like us. Finding a producer who would do these new songs justice was the final piece of the puzzle. Someone who could take them to the next level without losing the raw power that filled our rehearsal space night after night. David Briggs of Neil Young fame was considered, as we were lifetime fans of Neil's work, and David's instinct for capturing the unpolished, imperfect core of human performance was much aligned with our ragged sound. Don Dixon was also considered, having created more than a couple of our favourite tracks with REM and the Smithereens; his collection of song-based albums featured an undeniable attention to songwriting, craft, and arrangement. Perfect for Kurt's ever-evolving sense of melody and lyric. But ultimately, Butch Vig was our guy. First of all, there is no easier hang than a Butch Vig hang. The word "chill" doesn't even begin to define his Midwest Zen temperament. Just. Fucking. Cool. How he manages to amplify every musical element tenfold without making it feel like work is beyond me, but if the magic that was captured at Smart Studios with his first Nirvana session was any indication, we were well on our way to making something that would eclipse any and all expectations, including our own.

We began the process of booking a recording session with the assistance of our new partner in crime, John Silva, and the amazing guys at DGC. Butch was working on an album with a young Chicago band called Smashing Pumpkins at the time, so it was back to the barn day after day, woodshedding our collection of songs to be as ready as possible when the call came. We wouldn't have much time (or money) to mess around in the studio, maybe twelve days, so it was critical that these songs be produced promptly. Let's face it, we weren't producing a Genesis record here. And in order to capture the band's intensity in one take, we had to get our stuff together. Which we did. As unpleasant as it was to have to wait—another corn dog, another night on the couch with that stupid turtle—there was suddenly light at the end of the tunnel.

The conversation finally went to the choice of studio—if not the most crucial component, certainly a deciding factor in the output of every album. Recording studios are like lovers. No two are the same, and no one is flawless. Some you love to dislike, while others you despise. The trick is to locate one that will help you get out of yourself. Of course, Seattle had its share of fantastic studios, but there was talk of a place in Van Nuys, California, that had an amazing drum room, a classic recording console, and (most importantly) was cheap as fuck: Sound City. It looked like the perfect fit with its rough, no-nonsense, analog aesthetic. Not to mention that it was closer to the Hollywood Geffen offices, and I'm quite sure they wanted to keep an eye on us to make sure we weren't pulling another great rock and roll swindle like the Sex Pistols (which we pondered at one point). I don't blame them. The risk element was perhaps a notch higher than with our label partners Edie Brickell & New Bohemians, but little did they know, we meant business.

We began final preparations for our thousand-mile journey down to Los Angeles once the dates were finalised (May 2-19). We were ready to go after a few more rehearsals and some more boom box recordings of new song ideas. We're almost there. We needed petrol money. We hurriedly booked a last-minute gig at the OK Hotel, a small club in downtown Seattle, hoping that it would bring us enough money to fill our tanks and get us to Sound City without breaking down on the side of the road. It was April 17, 1991, and the little room was thankfully packed with sweaty kids eager to hear their beloved Nirvana tunes. "School," "Negative Creep," "About a

Girl," "Floyd the Barber"—these were all recognizable to the die-hard fans who cherished Nirvana's first album, Bleach, so we delivered them with our customary frantic abandon, pounding our instruments to within an inch of their lives while the crowd shouted every word. It was virtually transcendent, just like every previous Nirvana event I had seen. Rather than sticking to the tried-and-true back catalogue, we decided to try a new song that no one in the room had ever heard before that night. A song we wrote throughout the winter in that freezing little barn in Tacoma. Kurt approached the microphone and said, "This song is called 'Smells Like Teen Spirit.'" Crickets. He then went into the beginning riff, and the audience erupted as Krist and I burst into the song. Bodies jumping, people on top of people, a sea of denim and wet flannel in front of us. Reassuring, to say the least, and hardly the reception we'd hoped for. THIS WAS NO ORDINARY NEW SONG. This was unique. And maybe, just maybe, all of those months starving, freezing, longing for my friends and family back in Virginia while suffering the oppressive, grey Pacific Northwest winter in that filthy little apartment had been a test of my own strength and perseverance, with music being my only consolation and reward. Maybe it was enough. Maybe that sea of denim and wet flannel at the stage's edge was all I needed to survive. If it had all stopped there, I might have cheerfully returned to Virginia a changed man. I knew deep down that I wouldn't be returning as Kurt and I packed the ancient Datsun for the trip to Los Angeles. With my duffel bag over my shoulder, I took one final look at the tiny room I had called home for the past seven months, attempting to imprint every single detail in my mind so that I would never forget the memories or meaning of this place in my life. To ensure that whatever will come after these days was created here. And as I closed the door to go, my heart was bursting with a sense of finality, like a needle stabbing into your skin, leaving fuzzy memoirs of times that will never fade. A tiny mark here, a little mark there, indelible recollections of times gone by.

AFTER ALL, IT'S A FOREVER THING.

CHAPTER 6
THE DIVIDE

"Guess where we're swimming today," said Bryan Brown, my dear friend.

"I dunno... where?" I replied from the deathly hot bedroom of Pete Stahl's packed, air conditioner-less house in the San Fernando Valley.

"The house where Sharon Tate was killed by the Manson family."

I paused on the phone for a moment to comprehend this disturbing invitation before responding, "Cielo Drive? "Are you kidding me?" I knew precisely where he was referring to, having been somewhat familiar with America's most infamous and terrible killing spree since I was a teenager engrossed in the macabre world. This was almost too sinister to contemplate.

"Let's go."

1992 dawned with a debilitating, well-deserved hangover as I awoke in a sloppy hotel room the night before after spending New Year's Eve with the Red Hot Chili Peppers, Nirvana, Pearl Jam, and sixteen thousand other people at San Francisco's Cow Palace. Nirvana had ended our stormy, historic year with a brief West Coast tour of venues, all packed to the rafters with thousands of young punks eager to see these three up-and-coming bands in what was soon becoming a musical revolution. And the news that we had dethroned Michael Jackson at the top of the Billboard album rankings arrived on the same day that we were to appear on Saturday Night Live for the first time, January 11, 1992. This could have been the moment I realised my life would never be the same again. Saturday Night Live had been my favourite television show since I was a child, and I would stay up in my pyjamas every weekend to watch it, hoping to see my late-night TV heroes. But I wasn't just watching to see Dan Aykroyd, Gilda Radner, John Belushi, Laraine Newman, Bill Murray, Steve Martin, and Andy Kaufman's comedic genius; I was also intrigued by the vast spectrum of musical guests they welcomed every weekend. This was my education as a young musician, a master class in live performance by some of the world's most cutting-edge performers.

But if there was one performance that stood out from the rest and changed the trajectory of my life, it was the B-52s performing their single "Rock Lobster" in 1980.

THESE THREE MINUTES WERE NOT JUST A BAND PLAYING A SONG, BUT A RALLYING CRY TO ALL PEOPLE SUFFOCATING IN CONVENTIONALITY, AFRAID TO LET THEIR FREAK FLAG FLY, WHO WANTED TO CELEBRATE ALL OF LIFE'S BEAUTIFUL ECCENTRICITIES. My thoughts weren't quite this intricate when I was ten years old; I know that now. Even still, their pleasure in their oddness made me feel empowered. I knew I wanted to break free as I watched them dance their mess around in a goofy, frantic blur. I no longer desired to conform to the standard. Like the B-52s, I wanted to break away from the herd and live a life apart from the crowd. There comes a time in every child's life when freedom and individuality collide, directing you in the right direction, and this was mine. I'd be an outcast with a guitar who enjoyed both music and comedy. So there you have it. However, the opportunity to appear on SNL came at a difficult time for Nirvana. We hadn't seen each other since the end of our West Coast tour with the Red Hot Chili Peppers and Pearl Jam, and in that time we'd all gone our separate ways, fatigued after the seventy-five performances we'd done up to that point. I'd returned to Virginia, Krist had returned to Seattle, and Kurt had travelled to his new home in Los Angeles. When we met in New York City for the event, there was a sense of exhaustion, most notably with Kurt, and what I had imagined would be a triumphant reunion of the band, reunited to play the TV show that had altered my life, felt a little... wrong. There were fractures growing in our already unstable foundation, and a shaky foundation is not what you want when performing live on TV in front of millions of people waiting for their first view of the band that came out of nowhere to depose the "King of Pop" from his throne.

"Ladies and gentlemen . . . Nirvana."

Kurt began playing the intro to "Smells Like Teen Spirit," and my life flashed before my eyes, despite the fact that I'd played it every night in crowded theatres all around the world by then. This was where the B-52s had been stationed. Devo had been standing here.

This was the spot where David Bowie had stood. Every living star, from Bob Dylan to Mick Jagger, had stood on this stage to perform their songs for millions of young musicians like myself, who had stayed up long past their bedtime to see their heroes perform the songs that had changed their lives. I wanted to pass out. I felt like puking. I wanted to run away. But I blasted that drum start with everything I had and... broke a stick. Fuck.

I was now driving the song with one flat tire, three engines, and only one sandwich short of a picnic. I looked down at my lifelong friend Jimmy, who was serving as my show's drum tech, and we locked eyes in fear. It was one thing for this to happen at a Scream concert in front of 75 people; quite another when the entire globe was watching. Just keep playing, I reminded myself as I pounded the drums with a lifetime's worth of determination. I grabbed another stick with lightning speed and finished the song, surging with enough adrenaline to kill a horse but with enough pride to last a lifetime, imagining that maybe our performance was a rallying cry to a whole new generation of kids suffocating in conformity, afraid to let their freak flag fly, finally liberated to celebrate the beautiful eccentricities of life. Oh, and Weird Al called the dressing room that night to personally ask for permission to cover "Smells Like Teen Spirit" as well. We'd finally arrived. We split up after Saturday Night Live, reuniting two weeks later in Los Angeles to film the "Come As You Are" video before heading down to Australia and Japan for a three-and-a-half-week tour, another unimaginable experience to add to the list of things I never thought I'd live to see. Kurt was ill when I arrived in Los Angeles for the first day of the video filming. He appeared fragile and deflated, and the look in his eyes indicated that he had been high while away from the band.

In January 1991, I was in Los Angeles visiting a buddy when I learned Kurt was using heroin. I had never met anyone who had used heroin and understood very little about it, so I was taken aback. I'd only been in the band for three months and was living in a little flat with Kurt, and perhaps naively, I didn't think he'd do something like that. Kurt told me that he did not use heroin on a regular basis, but only once. "I hate needles," he continued, trying to reassure me that I hadn't suddenly woken up and travelled across the country to live with a stranger who turned out to be a junkie. I trusted him because I knew nothing about the medicine. In any case, he'd never be able to keep such a secret from me. So I reasoned. Someone had pills one night in Olympia while I was out drinking with pals. Some kind of prescription pain reliever. "Take one with a few beers, and you'll be super buzzed," that's what I was informed. Even that made me anxious, so I limited myself to drinks, but I did notice Kurt took two or three with his drink. It frightened me. I was always hesitant to take anything for fear of the consequences of taking too much, but I had pals back in Virginia who would always test the limits to see how far they could go. Kurt was this way in every aspect, I discovered.

I FINALLY FELT THE DEPARTURE. Those who did and those who did not participated. That difference widened as our world expanded. Nirvana consisted of three distinct persons, each with his own quirks and peculiarities that contributed to the distinct sound we generated when we strapped on our instruments, but outside of the music, we lived our own lives, each extremely different from the others. Kurt's frailty struck me as we shot the video, and I was frightened not only for his health but also for the tour we were about to embark on, which would take us to the other side of the earth, far from the people we loved and needed the most. I couldn't see how we'd make it through another crazy schedule of show after show, airport after airport, and hotel after hotel, especially considering his health, but we did. It's still difficult for me to watch "Come As You Are" knowing what Kurt was going through at the time. Despite the fact that our views are blurred by camera effects and washed-out Super 8 film projected onto raw surfaces, I see three people entering what would become a period of turbulence that we would feel for years.Tan, nourished, and content, I went right back to Virginia after my week on Fantasy Island with Mr. Roarke and Tattoo, my first "vacation" since I was a youngster, but with this newfound financial freedom came increased obligations. The unthinkable has finally occurred. I was wealthy. There could be solace after a lifetime of watching my mother juggle many jobs and count every dime. I stayed pretty frugal, oblivious to the immensity of what was to come, as my father (who had recovered from the disowning) soon reminded me, "You know this isn't going to last, right? You must regard each check as if it is the last one you will ever write." This is still, arguably, the best piece of advice he or anyone has ever given me.

Though that didn't stop me from going straight to the motorbike showroom and purchasing matching Yamaha V-Maxes for Jimmy and me, it did induce a dread of bankruptcy right away, so in the broad scheme of things, my life remained pretty unchanged. As was our custom, we dispersed in various directions. Krist returned to Seattle and purchased a warm, cosy home in the Green Lake neighbourhood to the north of the city. Kurt moved to Los Angeles and found a charming modest flat in an old Hollywood building. I bought a house in Corolla, North Carolina, only blocks from the ocean, because I wasn't ready to commit to living full-time in Seattle. The Outer Banks, only a few hours from Northern Virginia, was the ideal place for me to invest in real estate, not only because of its raw natural beauty, with high dunes and wild horses running along the wide beaches, but also because of its proximity to home, allowing me to share my profits with my mother and sister.

BUT "IDLE HANDS ARE THE DEVIL'S PLAYGROUND," I'VE BEEN TOLD.

As we all settled into our new lifestyles, the schism reappeared. We were no longer crammed together in tight trucks or shared hotel rooms for months on end, and we were finally free to live the life we had always imagined, for better or worse. We had witnessed the world transform around us, a swirl of flashbulbs and near-riots at every turn, but now that the hurricane of lunacy had passed, we were free to create our own realities however we saw fit. As the band's anonymous drummer, I was fortunate to go through life almost unnoticed, rarely stopped in public, and typically just asked, "Are you Dave Navarro?" It was almost as if I were on the outside looking in, seeing this all unfold from afar, enjoying the perks of "making it" without having to answer for it. That could not be said for Kurt, whose face was now on the cover of every magazine, in every MTV News episode, and his voice could be heard on every FM radio station from coast to coast, a life sentence that most people are not equipped to negotiate. We retired to our corners, nursed our wounds, and closed the book on the year punk came of age. With nothing but time until Nirvana's next tour, I bounced from surfing in North Carolina to revisiting my old DC haunts with lifelong friends, to recording my primitive songs in Barrett Jones' basement in Seattle, to flying down to L.A. to reconnect with my old friends Pete and Franz from Scream, who had stayed there since the day I left to join Nirvana, starting new lives (and a new band, Wool) after Scream's demise. What was supposed to be a week on the floor of their small Valley house grew into at least a month, waking up every morning in the sweltering summer heat. The house was a red-hot pizza oven by midday, so the only way to escape the desert heat was to find a pool and spend the afternoon swimming in someone else's oasis, which was my pal Bryan Brown's specialty. My excitement was tinged with dread as we approached the mansion on Cielo Drive, realising that the sick fascination I'd always felt with this house was going to be met with the unsettling reality of stepping within its cursed walls. We rang the gatebell, drove into the driveway, stepped out of the car, and there it was, precisely as it had been in every crime scene photo I had ever placed my youthful, inquisitive eyes on. My spine was chilled. We knocked on the front door—THAT front door. We were taken inside, but I didn't need a guide to show me around; it was almost as if I had been there before. I turned the corner into the living room and was met by a terrifying shock wave. The stone fireplace, the wooden beams, the small loft... everything was precisely as it had been on that dreadful night of August 9, 1969. Except for one thing: in the middle of the room stood a big recording console. Nine Inch Nails were setting a new standard in this venue.

I hadn't met Nine Inch Nails, but I had seen them perform live. My teenage soundtrack included Throbbing Gristle, Psychic TV, Einstürzende Neubauten, and Current 93, among others. I really liked NIN's first album, Pretty Hate Machine. With the band's violent electro-tension and dark lyrical themes, it was only natural that they would record their second album at the Manson mansion. As messed up as it was, it was a great fit, and they recorded some of their most emotional songs there, including "March of the Pigs," "Hurt," and "Closer." I've always believed that the environment in which you record influences the outcome of the music, and each time I hear one of these tracks, I'm confident it's true. There's a sense of pain and despair in these songs that was undoubtedly permeated by spiritual osmosis. Or Trent Reznor's anguish and despair. I didn't know him well, but he struck me as a wonderful artist and a gentle soul. Like another gentle and creative musician I knew, he used music to identify the demons that tortured his spirit. After a time, the house's pervasive mood clearly threw a pall over the spirit of the environment, one with which I couldn't connect or jibe at all. I was all too familiar with the feeling of gloom, fragility, and agony, so I went to the pool not only to cool down, but also to wash away the feeling I had standing in that living room.

The darker side of music was always something I was sonically drawn to, but I realised it wasn't who I was as a person. To me, music has always signified brightness and vitality. Even joy. I wanted to celebrate finding a way out of the tunnel. I wanted to wave my freak flag. I didn't want to go into hiding. I could see how some would go in the opposite direction, possibly revisiting unsolved traumas, but I finally felt free of mine, and that felt good. I needed to find calm, whether in the sand dunes of North Carolina or the quiet of Virginia's placid suburbs, and with the increased freedom that success had given me, I was going to spend my time looking for it. The rest of my days in LA were spent driving around in a rented white Volkswagen Cabriolet convertible (yes, I had a thing for convertibles at the time), swimming in strangers' pools, jamming with friends, and calling the airlines every few days to change my return ticket to Seattle, extending my stay on Pete's scorching-hot floor for a little more summer and a little more distance before returning to the grey skies up north. I guess I knew what was waiting for me there deep down.

Finally, at the last minute, I decided it was time to leave and tossed everything I owned into the back of the Cabriolet, raced to LAX in the hopes of making my flight on time. I knew nothing about the convoluted web of busy freeways that crisscrossed the vast city, so I began speeding through the Valley at unsafe speeds, hoping to be heading in the general direction of at least one access ramp. I noticed one only metres ahead of me as I screamed around a corner, so I twisted the wheel to the right as hard as I could and... BAM!

I slammed into a towering curb at 45 mph, which not only dragged the front axle out from beneath the car but also triggered the airbag (which I had no idea it had), which detonated ten inches from my face like a stick of dynamite. I got out of the car, bruised and pummelling, coughing from the smoke powder that blasted out when it smacked me in the face like a canvas bat, and dialled 911 for a tow truck. (Do not be misled by those safety advertisements, ladies and gentlemen. Although a saviour, an airbag is hardly a lovely silky cushion. That crap will fuck you up like a Mike Tyson right uppercut.) The welt on my left eye began to grow like a gigantic balloon once the truck came and the driver inspected the damage, and he ruled the automobile totaled.

I took a cab back to Pete's house with a black eye and my tail between my legs for another week's stay, having utterly damaged a perfectly nice Cabriolet convertible that cost only $12 a day. The extra week in Los Angeles allowed me to rest my black eye while simultaneously planning my next steps. That gap between the three of us, and whether or not we could bridge it this time. The world had finally heard about Nirvana. We were the out-of-the-ordinary freaks that the entire world was suddenly watching. Could we make it?

Kurt was discovered to be at a recovery facility in Los Angeles. I was concerned, but not shocked. This was a good sign for me. While I was reuniting with old acquaintances on the other side of town, perhaps he was finding some light and calm of his own. I had never met anyone who had gone to rehab, so I assumed it was a quick fix, like an appendectomy or having your tonsils removed. Aside from my father's issues with alcohol, I had no idea what addiction was like. To be sure, I was unaware of Kurt's depths. I hadn't realised that the mending required to break free from the grips of this type of illness takes a lifetime—if you can hold on and stay out of the abyss.

THERE WAS STILL SO MUCH TO BE EXCITED ABOUT. WE'D ONLY JUST STARTED.

CHAPTER 7
THE HEARTBREAKER

"Dave, there's a phone call for you."

The studio engineer handed me the handset at the end of the long, curly line, and to my astonishment, it was Ron Stone calling, an acquaintance of my management we referred to as "Old School" because of his days working with legends like Bonnie Raitt and Neil Young. We'd never worked together, so it was rare for him to call me personally, but what he'd called to convey was even more unique.

"Tom Petty wants to know if you'll play drums for him on Saturday Night Live . . ."

"Wait, what?" I asked, perplexed. Why me? And he's phoning me when he could have any drummer in the world?" We're talking about Tom Petty, America's favourite Floridian, the personification of grassroots, working-class cool, the voice behind decades of classic rock singles like "Breakdown," "American Girl," "Refugee," and "Free Fallin'."

His music was the soundtrack to a thousand hickeys, tunes oozing with feel and rhythm, and he was calling the guy who could only play the drums one way: on or off? It made no sense at all. Tom was about to release one of his most renowned solo albums, Wildflowers, and had lately parted ways with original Heartbreakers drummer Stan Lynch, so he needed someone to occupy the drum stool for a promotional Saturday Night Live performance. Any invitation to visit the renowned television studios of SNL, my favourite show, was a privilege (fun fact: as of this writing, SNL is still on the air). I was on fourteen times (more than any other musician), yet I still didn't get it. Petty was one of my favourite artists of all time, a musical hero to millions of young suburban misfits like myself, so the idea that he even recognized my name was surreal. Not to mention that I hadn't touched a drum set, let alone played live, since Nirvana's demise. I paused, taken aback by such a flattering proposal, and gently requested a day or two to consider it. To say the least, my mind was in a different place at the moment. I DID NEED TO CONSIDER THINGS.

I knew the day would come when I'd be asked to cross this bridge, to move on with my life after a year of sorrow, but I wasn't expecting the cause to be this. I hung up the phone in the studio control room, where I was standing with a guitar over my neck, and returned to what I was doing when the phone call came in: recording what would unknowingly become the first Foo Fighters record. I was lost after Kurt died. We were all. With our world being ripped out from under us in such a rapid and traumatic manner, it was difficult to find any direction or beacon to assist guide us through the fog of enormous pain and loss. And because Kurt, Krist, and I were all linked by music, any song seemed bittersweet. What had once been my greatest delight had now become my greatest anguish, and I not only put my instruments away, but I also shut off the radio, afraid that even the faintest music would provoke paralysing grief. It was the first time in my life that I had turned down music. I couldn't bear the thought of it breaking my heart again. I felt like a fish caught in a little bowl for months after his death, feverishly swimming back and forth all day but never really getting anywhere. I was just twenty-five years old and had an entire life ahead of me, but I felt like it had all ended. The prospect of putting my drum equipment onstage behind just another face was not only unpleasant, but also depressing. I was too young to die, yet too old to begin again. Sure, I could join another band, but I'd always be known as "that guy from Nirvana," and I knew deep down that nothing could ever equal what Nirvana had given to the world. That kind of incident happens only once in a lifetime.

After months of spinning my wheels in suffocating bouts of introspection, I decided I needed to get away from Seattle and clear my head, so I travelled to a corner of the world that I have always adored, a place of serenity and natural beauty where I hoped to find some healing from my broken life back home: the Ring of Kerry. The Ring of Kerry, a beautiful, secluded location in southwestern Ireland, is a return to what the earth must have been like thousands of years ago, before man carved it into concrete lots and busy thoroughfares. There is a peace and tranquillity there that I so urgently needed to review my life and start anew, with miles of the greenest fields overlooking coastal scenery and seaside settlements. I'd been there before, spending a week with my mother and sister driving from Dublin to Dingle before Nirvana's 1992 Reading Festival appearance (our final performance in the UK), and felt a connection to that landscape like no other. Maybe it was my mother's Irish heritage, or maybe it was the slower pace of life, which reminded me of the rural sections of Virginia where I used to go hunting as a youngster, but whatever it was, I felt at ease in its solitude and calm. That was just what I needed right now. I observed a teenage hitchhiker in the distance one day while I was guiding my rental car past the potholes and deep ruts of a distant country road. I could tell this guy was a rocker from his long, greasy hair and enormous parka, and he desperately needed a transport to his goal because he was miles from the next town. As I got closer, I intended to pick him up and give him a ride, until I noticed something that immediately changed my mind. He was dressed casually in a Kurt Cobain T-shirt. I rushed passed with my head down, hoping he didn't recognize me when a wave of worry hit me like a jolt from an electric chair. My hands were trembling, and I felt physically sick, dizzy in the grips of a debilitating panic attack. Kurt's face stared back at me, almost as if to remind me that no matter how far I ran, I could never escape the past. This was the moment when everything changed.

I returned to the United States and thought it was time to get back to work. Without a band or a solid plan in place, I went back to where I felt most at ease: recording songs by myself. With the help of two cassette recorders, an old guitar, and several pots and pans, I learnt to do this by accident when I was twelve years old. My method was straightforward: record a guitar part on one cassette, remove that tape, insert it into cassette player number two, push Play, record myself playing "drums" along with the guitar part on another cassette, and so on. Without realising it, I was multitracking. I'd create crazy songs about my dog, my school, and Ronald Reagan, but I was thrilled by the process and did it frequently. What's the best part? No one ever knew since I was terrified of letting anyone hear my prepubescent shriek.

I was familiar with the concept of laying down all of the instruments myself, systematically layering guitars, drums, and vocals as I had done as a child, by the time I started hanging out and recording with my friend Barrett Jones on the eight-track machine in his Virginia basement studio, though the RadioShack cassette players had been replaced with Barrett's professional reel-to-reel equipment. I didn't want to impose (and I didn't have the money to pay him for engineering), so I'd wait until the conclusion of someone else's session and ask, "Is there any extra tape at the end of the reel?" "I'd like to try something..." Knowing that this was a hefty task (and that I had already smoked most of his cannabis), I would sprint from one instrument to the next, doing only one take on the drums, one take on guitar, and one take on bass to avoid wasting any more of Barrett's time or generosity. Then I'd go home and replay my small experiment, envisioning what I could achieve if I had more than fifteen minutes to record a song. Barrett moved to Seattle and we got a house together, and his studio was in MY basement, so I took advantage of the proximity and began writing songs that, while rudimentary and not yet ready for the public to hear, were a little more evolved. "Alone and Easy Target," "Floaty," "Weenie Beenie," "Exhausted," and "I'll Stick Around" were just a few of the scores of songs we recorded in our modest basement on rainy days, and I was gradually accumulating what would eventually become the Foo Fighters' catalogue. Nirvana was in full flow at the time, and we didn't need any help in the songwriting department, so I kept the songs to myself, recalling the old drummer joke, "What was the last thing the drummer said before getting kicked out of the band?" "Hey, guys, I wrote a song that I think we should play!!"

With nothing to lose and nowhere to run, I returned from Ireland and booked six days at Robert Lang Studios, a twenty-four-track studio down the street from my house in Richmond Beach, a state-of-the-art facility built into the side of a massive hill overlooking the Puget Sound. I'd previously recorded there, including Nirvana's final session, where we recorded our final song, "You Know You're Right," earlier that year. Robert Lang, the studio's eclectic, eccentric owner, decided to build a recording facility beneath his house in the early 1970s and spent fifteen years digging deeper and deeper into the hill, hauling thousands of dump trucks worth of dirt away and creating what can only be described as a gigantic concrete bunker with a great collection of vintage microphones. The materials he decided to employ in the tracking rooms, however, distinguished him from other studios. His rooms, instead of the soft absorption of natural wood and acoustically corrected baffles, featured the merciless reflection of rough stone, which produced a considerably more "live" sound. It was the dark green Chinese marble that drew Nirvana to the studio, as Bob showed us a little block that he was persuaded housed a vision of a saintlike person, a halo, a dove, and the resurrection descending during our initial visit. That's when Krist Novoselic and I said, "Oh, we're DEFINITELY recording here... this guy is WILD." Not to mention how near it was to my house that I could drive there on my lawn mower-powered go-kart.

I made a reservation for October 17 to 22, 1994, and began to plan. I chose fifteen songs from the innumerable recordings Barrett and I had produced over the years that I thought were the best, collected the gear, and devised a plan: four songs a day for four days, with the last two days for vocals and mixing. I could actually pull it off if I recorded at the same tempo I always did, racing from instrument to instrument, doing only one or two takes before moving on to the next. I established a calendar, picking which songs to record on which days, and rehearsed like crazy, knowing I didn't have much time. Six days in the studio felt like an eternity, but I needed to show to myself that I could fulfil the goal I had set for myself, which was the entire point of this new project.

Barrett and I loaded the gear in the morning of Monday, made coffee, gathered sounds, and were ready to push Record by noon. A new song called "This Is a Call" was up first, and I blasted through the drums in one take, instantly strapped on the guitar, and finished it swiftly before going on to the bass for one run. The instrumental was completed in 45 minutes. "I'll Stick Around" came next. Same routine: drums, guitar, bass, and finished in 45 minutes. Then "Big Me," then "Alone and Easy Target"... at the end of the first day, we'd completed our four-song quota with time to spare, and my lofty ambition no longer seemed so lofty. I truly felt... well, good. To me, this was more than just a recording session; it was profoundly healing. Life's continuance. This was what I needed to defibrillate my heart and restore it to a normal beat, an electric pulse to rekindle my love of music. Aside from simply picking up an instrument and feeling active or prolific, I could once again see through the windshield rather than in the rearview mirror. By the end of the week, I had not only completed the fifteen songs (actually recording them in the order of the eventual album), but I had also agreed to play with Tom Petty on Saturday Night Live, which was a step back into my former life but one I was no longer afraid to take. There was finally light at the end of the tunnel. These were not intended to be long-term life goals; rather, they were tiny steps forward. There was no vision for what was to come. Not quite yet. I took the master tape of Barrett's rough mixes to a tape duplication shop in downtown Seattle, where I decided to make a hundred cassette copies of my new project, intending to give them to friends, family, and anyone else who was curious about what "that guy from Nirvana" had been up to since the band's demise. I had kept my songs a secret for much of my life, but now I was ready to share them with the world because I was more proud of them than anything else I had ever recorded. Barrett's incredible producing talents provided more than simply musical pleasure; it also provided emotional satisfaction. I had eventually surfaced with the exaggerated gasp of someone who had been held underwater for too long.

Despite the fact that I had played every instrument on that cassette (with the exception of one guitar track played by my friend Greg Dulli from the Afghan Whigs, whom I handed a guitar to one day while he was at the studio), I was mortified by the thought of it being a "solo" effort. I couldn't envision "the Dave Grohl Experience" being a moniker that would have people rushing to the record stores, and I knew that the Nirvana connection would undoubtedly overshadow any listener's neutrality. So I chose a more incognito path, drawing influence from Police drummer Stewart Copeland and his 1980 "solo" project Klark Kent. To avoid jeopardising the Police's career at the moment, Stewart opted to record under the alias Klark Kent, playing all of the instruments himself, exactly as I had done. That mystery appealed to me. I borrowed a simple phrase from a book I was reading at the time, Above Top Secret, which was a collection of UFO encounter reports and accounts from the military dating back to the early 1940s. I found a phrase that the military used as a moniker for these unexplained blazing balls of light in a chapter about unidentified objects over Europe and the Pacific during World War II and thought it was just weird enough for me. It sounded not only like a bunch of people, but almost like a gang: Foo Fighters.

I designed the simple cassette inlay that would be inserted into the case with each tape, selecting the font and paper colour, writing the credits and song titles, and leaving the tape duplicating facility feeling ten feet tall, knowing that my gift would be ready by the end of the week. I felt like I was walking on air. The prize was straightforward: I had done it myself. While I waited, I packed my bags and prepared to go to Los Angeles for my rehearsal with Tom Petty. I'd been sent the two songs that would be performed on the show, "You Don't Know How It Feels" and "Honey Bee," and I was listening to them over and over again, trying to recall all of Steve Ferrone's magnificent drum riffs and lock into his flawless feel. My manner was a million miles distant from his comfortable flow, so I concentrated on finding some Zen to calm my typical anarchic method. But it wasn't simply the music that made me nervous. I was set to meet Tom Petty for the first time. The band and staff greeted me with the most down-to-earth, genuine, and polite welcome when I arrived at the large practice space in the San Fernando Valley just outside of Hollywood, a temple of paisley and incense with a massive totem pole at one end of the room. With their casual swagger and mild Southern accents, the Heartbreakers were the embodiment of cool; they made me feel at home and appreciated, doing their best to neutralise any nerves they clearly knew I was experiencing. They were genuine rock stars, after all, and I'm sure they had this effect on most people, but they wanted to make me feel at ease with their friendliness and understanding. As we talked, I put up my drum set on the riser and gave my kick drum a loud WHACK, which made the entire room jump, and they turned to each other and laughed, almost as if to say, "Holy shit, what have we gotten ourselves into?"

After that, there was Tom. He was just how I had imagined him to be, absolutely laid-back and effortlessly cool, and when he said hello, the voice of a thousand high school dances flowed like thick molasses from his mouth. Any nerves I had from this rock and roll fantasy camp reverie had evaporated within a few minutes, and we began to play. I couldn't suppress my excitement, so I suppose I gave it a little more muscle than usual, because the band was nearly cringing from the cannon-level volume of my drums. In between takes, we spent the afternoon jamming, hanging out, and informally getting to know each other, and by the end of the day, they had made me feel like an honorary Heartbreaker. I had the impression that we were a band. And it was a sensation I hadn't had in a long time. We gathered a week later for soundcheck at the Saturday Night Live studios, which is usually on Thursday. This is when the SNL team adjusts the sound levels and does the camera blocking. You first soundcheck and rehearse, playing each song two or three times in the control room to get the stage monitors dialled in and everything sounding right, then you break for lunch and return an hour later for camera blocking, where the director rehearses his camera angles and moves for when they go live. With decades of experience behind them, this is usually an easy affair, with only a few takes, and they nail it with ease.

However, after the initial camera blocking take, the stage director approached my enormous drum kit and asked, "Ummm, Dave... is there any way to move that rack to just a few inches to the left?" We're having trouble seeing your face." I was terrified and ashamed in front of these heroes, and I didn't know what to say. I didn't want to upset anyone because I was just a humble visitor along for the ride, so why the fuck would they care about seeing me? This was a Tom Petty concert! I looked to Tom for advice, and he said, "Don't let them tell you what to do, kid." "Stand your ground," I said uneasily, "Ummm... no, that's where it goes, I'd rather not." A stagehand emerged seconds later with a smaller microphone for the drum, hoping for a clearer shot for the cameras. We sang the song one more time, and the stage director reappeared, this time approaching Tom. "Excuse me, Mr. Petty, is there any way we can move you just a few feet to the right?" That was absolute boldness. This guy has a lot of balls. On that iconic platform, you could have heard a fucking pin drop, a stage Tom was surely familiar with, having graced it four times before. "No, man, we worked all day to make it sound good, and it finally does." If you move anything, it'll mess everything up." The stage director begged and pleaded until Tom finally threw up his hands in the air and said, "Fine. But I'm telling you, it's going to screw everything up... "

We counted into the second take after they repositioned Tom's monitors and microphone a few feet to the right. As Tom approached the microphone to sing the first line, an ear-piercing shriek of feedback pierced our ears, causing us all to stop playing and plug our ears. Oh fuck... here it comes, I thought.

Tom was enraged, but only in the way that Tom Petty could be. He never lost his temper, simply looking at the stage director and saying, "You. "Please come here." The poor guy slinked up to the stage, aware that he had maybe made a career-defining error, and Tom asked, "What did I just tell you?" in his trademark Southern drawl. The director apologised and said he would immediately reposition the equipment, but Tom added, "No, I want you to tell me what I just told you." The director then repeated Tom's admonition word for word, prompting Tom to respond, "That's right, now put it back." It wasn't a scolding or a shaming to me; it was a man who had fought his entire life for what he believed in, suffering endless hardships and demoralizing industry nonsense, letting the world know that you couldn't fuck with him. At that moment, I was proud to be his drummer—not Nirvana's drummer, but Tom Petty's drummer. And, as if I hadn't already admired him, I now admired him even more.

The show was fantastic. We rocked both songs with rhythm and passion, and after only a week and a half of knowing each other, I was starting to feel strangely at ease within the band's laid-back dynamic, something I had never felt in the three and a half years I was in Nirvana. Nirvana's awkward dysfunction certainly made a lot of noise, but the sense of family and community in the Heartbreakers' camp looked far healthier and less chaotic. This was just what I needed to calm my past traumas, and it served as a wonderful reminder that music does signify love, life, and celebration. This was the ideal one-off to get me back on my feet, I reasoned. Then Tom asked whether I was interested in doing it again. This was a game-changer. An unexpected turn of events that enhanced the experience while also making it more perplexing. How could I ever turn down such an opportunity? I never imagined I was worthy or capable of such an offer, but gosh, it felt wonderful to be asked. He asked me to think about it as we stood in the narrow hallway outside the tiny dressing room after our performance, and I thanked him profusely, still amazed that I was speaking with the man who wrote the classic "Runnin' Down a Dream," a song about following life's crooked path with all of its twists and turns, never knowing where it may take you. I returned home and picked up my hundred tapes, carefully putting them in a cardboard box that I proceeded to load into my pickup as if it were the first time I was bringing a newborn home from the hospital. Had I left my heart with Tom Petty in New York City? Or was it in that cardboard box full of new cassettes? I WAS STANDING AT A CROSSROADS.

The sensation I had with the Heartbreakers was so satisfying, so soothing, and so needed at the time, yet I knew deep down that I would never truly be a Heartbreaker. They were linked by decades of history, and as charming, warm, and gracious as they were, I would always be "that guy from Nirvana," a moniker I was clearly honoured to hold, but it came with some pretty heavy baggage. I adored Tom's music and would have had a ball playing his tunes night after night, but... they weren't mine. We chatted on the phone once again, and Tom explained that they had a really comfortable tour. I'd have my own bus, and the scheduling would be much more casual than the arduous van excursions I was used to. Everything sounded so wonderful. It's almost too perfect. I was twenty-five years old and still hungry, unwilling to settle for a "sure thing." I still had the restless energy of a teen, motivated to thrive in the unknown, even if it was scary at times. As a result, I politely rejected and determined that the cardboard box in the back of my vehicle held the key to a new life. It was far from certain, but nothing ever is.

CHAPTER 8
SWEET VIRGINIA

"I'm going to need some privacy, so... nothing under four hundred acres," I declared confidently.

"Wow!" exclaimed my real estate agent, Connie. "Okay! Let me get started on that, and I'll get back to you as soon as possible with some listings!" To be honest, the surprise in her speech caught me off guard. This didn't seem like such an unreasonable request when I was looking for a house to live in, a guesthouse for the band, and a barn to convert into a recording studio so that I could ride off into the sunset, living out my dream of being completely self-sufficient in a sleepy Virginia town. On the other hand, I had no notion how big an acre was. My time in Seattle had finally come to an end after seven years. I'd arrived as a complete stranger, lived in filthy desolation and emotional isolation, found my groove with a new group that went on to become the largest band in the world, had it all ripped out from under me, and had to start over. A lifetime in and of itself. I had left my heart in Virginia, my forever home, as much as I loved the city and the friends I had formed there over the years. Growing up in its suburbs among the rolling hills and huge oak trees, I never imagined myself living anyplace else, no matter how desperately I wanted to escape its quiet monotony and predictability as a child. I'd always assumed I'd end up back where I started.

In the fall of 1996, as we began recording the Foo Fighters' second album, The Colour and the Shape (our most popular record to this day), at Bear Creek Studios outside of Seattle, I realised that my time in the Pacific Northwest was coming to an end. Not only had I always felt like a visitor, just another transplant in a city fiercely protective of its precious roots, but my first marriage was in its final throes, casting a shadow over our recording sessions in the deep woods as the darkest winter months lay ahead (themes that run throughout the lyrics of that album). The fire that Seattle had lit in my heart was dying, and no matter how hard I fanned the flames, I would never be able to rekindle what had been. It's time to move on, I reasoned. I no longer belong here. Or, as Pat Smear famously put it, "too many ghosts."

But, before returning east to the area where I felt most at home, I decided to spend a year in Los Angeles (my version of The Lost Weekend), getting a feel for my newfound emancipation mere blocks away from the sinking ship full of mud wrestlers from which I had barely escaped. I could no longer live on dollar bills and canned baked beans because I could now afford my own house (and food). I rented a cosy two-bedroom house just down the street from the Sunset Strip, which I proceeded to enjoy with reckless abandon, no longer bound by anything or anyone. Although the making of our second album left us on shaky ground (original drummer William Goldsmith quit after I re-recorded his drum tracks, but was thankfully replaced by the overly qualified Taylor Hawkins, and Pat Smear temporarily left soon after), we had now become a band. I needed to let off some steam after overcoming the difficulties of recording our second album. I felt liberated in a way that made me want to indulge in everything I had been putting off for years. And I didn't hold back. Taylor Hawkins, my new partner in crime, introduced me to the considerably less pompous and far more lethal mix of Coors Light and tequila after years of swilling pitchers of heavy Hefeweizen and the sophisticated microbrews of the Pacific Northwest. Any hesitancy I'd originally felt about letting my hair down had vanished, leaving a trail of Patrón bottles and chewed-up lime wedges in its wake. Former Scream vocalist Pete Stahl had obtained a job at the Viper Room, a hedonistic pit of vice conveniently located down the street from my house, at the time. This became my nightly haunt, generally ending with me drinking until the sun came up in a cottage full of derelicts after the last call. That year was, to put it mildly, memorable. But after a year of gluttonous excess, I recognized that this was not the sunset I was supposed to ride out into. I set my sights on a more wholesome horizon: rural Virginia's nirvana. I flew back east to meet Connie, and we started our house hunt in the picturesque small town of Leesburg, constructed in 1740 and only an hour from the cosmopolitan whirl of Washington, DC, with beautiful old buildings on every corner and stone walls lining miles of meandering horse country. This was a throwback to my childhood, as I had spent many summers looking for Civil War bullets while dove hunting in the sweltering heat, and winters placing goose decoys in the hardened, icy mud before sunrise, waiting for the flocks to arrive from a pit dug into the cold earth, hoping to bring home dinner. As we drove to our first listing, those memories flowed over me, but Connie gave one caveat: "Now, this first property is a bit smaller than what you were looking for, but the house itself is gorgeous, and it has the guesthouse and barn you were looking for." "How much smaller?" I inquired, a little dismayed. "It's about one hundred acres," she said. How about a hundred acres? That is insignificant! I pondered. On barely a hundred acres, how could I possibly vanish and play music into the wee hours of the morning with my band? "Well, we're here," I explained. "I suppose we should go check it out..."

I was dwarfed by the huge columns that towered overhead as I stood on the front porch of this immaculate, two-hundred-year-old mansion that was once a fox hunting lodge, and as I looked out at the expanse of lush green fields below, I realised why my real estate agent was in shock on that first call. A hundred acres was the size of a goddamned farm. What about 400 acres? That's a whole fucking county. I wasn't a surveyor, and I was embarrassed by my lack of agricultural knowledge, but equally humbled by the awe-inspiring beauty of the property that lay before me, its perimeter lined with trees as a natural boundary, flowing down to a little river in the distance. Oh my god! I pondered. What did I get myself into?

We walked through the main mansion (which reminded me a little too much of the White House, which I know I'll never live in), then over to the guest house, where it instantly dawned on me that this was all wrong. Here I was, thirty years old, about to literally "buy the farm," as they say, as if my glorious life of music and adventure had come to an end, about to ride off into the sunset, never to be seen or heard from again. Not to mention that the fucking guesthouse was twice the size of the modest house I grew up in an hour away, a house in which my mother, sister, and I were perfectly content to share our entire lives. But the barn seemed appealing. With its towering ceilings and massive square footage, more than enough area to fit a whole orchestra, I could easily see it being a world-class recording facility. But I wasn't quite ready to relax just yet. MORE WORK REMAINED TO BE DONE.

Connie drove me to a few more postings, all of which were between 250 and 400 acres. ("Would you like to walk the property line?"

she'd inquire. No thanks), but it was pointless because my mind was made up. This pipe dream would have to be postponed. Maybe when life slows down and I have a lovely family to share it with, I'll appreciate this home, rural Americana thing. But not just yet. I eventually settled on a more reasonable house on one and a half acres outside of historic former Town Alexandria, only a few miles from my former neighbourhood, and started building on what would become the basement recording studio where the Foo Fighters would operate for years to come. We'd recently been released from our contract with Capitol Records due to a "key man clause" that stated that if Capitol Records president Gary Gersh (an old friend who'd also signed Nirvana to Geffen years before) left, we had the option to leave as well, a provision that had been written and accepted due to our long history together. His leaving was an exceptional stroke of luck, and we chose to follow him, giving us entire independence, which most bands never have despite being locked into a deal for numerous albums.

The beauty of this was that we were no longer bound to be a band. We didn't have to do anything, but we wanted to, to demonstrate our sincerity. It had been a difficult few years since our first record, with constant touring, trying to find our legs, battling the sophomore slump, and losing a few members along the way, but we always persevered because we genuinely enjoyed playing together. Nate's twenty-four-hour fast in the spring of 1998 was the one time I actually considered quitting. Nate called while I was at my mother's house in Virginia to tell me that his heart wasn't in it any longer and that he felt more at home with his former band, Sunny Day Real Estate, which was organising a reunion. This one captivated me. William was never made out for the band's energy and drive, Pat was "over it" when he departed, Franz was a great old buddy but it never clicked, but Nate? The guy who helped me put this whole thing together? I'd had enough and angrily answered, "Okay, well, I'm sick of teaching people these fucking songs, so when I find a guy, YOU have to teach them." We said our goodbyes, but I knew the Foo Fighters were over without Nate. I couldn't take another resignation, and it was starting to feel eerily like the solo project I'd never wanted to be. That night, I went out drinking with my best friend Jimmy at my favourite low-rent barbecue spot, Ribsters, and proceeded to get blackout drunk, crying in my Jack and Cokes, defeated by another blow to my life's biggest passion. When I got home, I passed out in my old bedroom, my mind spinning like a top, and was awakened the next morning by my mother's voice murmuring gently outside my door, "David?" Nate's on the phone... I grabbed the massive cordless phone, extended the long antenna, and hissed, "Helloooo..." Nate then apologised, explaining that he'd had a short lack of judgement and that he didn't want to leave the band after all. To say I felt relieved would be an understatement; I was nearly reborn. We cried, saying "I love you, man," hung up the phone, and I slid back into bed, realising I'd pissed it the night before.

Taylor and I planned a cross-country trip from Los Angeles to Virginia, just two young men in a black Chevy Tahoe, flying down the interstate on a mad coast-to-coast journey, listening to classic rock at dangerous volumes. Taylor and I had grown nearly inseparable since he joined the band the previous year, becoming devious partners in crime from the start. We would run into one another backstage at festivals all over the world during his time as Alanis Morissette's drummer, and our chemistry was so clear that Alanis herself once asked him, "What are you going to do when Dave asks you to be his drummer?" We were a hyperactive flurry of Parliament Lights and air drumming wherever we went, so there was no one I would have rather enjoyed this psychotic safari with than Taylor. We planned a few stops along the route, including visits to Taylor's grandma and Pantera's strip club (the latter being a big priority), but for the most part it was a straight 2,600-mile drive back to my hometown. (When Taylor arrived, he did his best Bruce Springsteen impression, serenading me with the Boss's legendary hymn of the same name. Only the time he performed the Cheers theme on a piano in the midst of a packed Costco was funnier.) I threw one last goodbye party in my little canyon bungalow, put my modest goods into a stack of U-Haul boxes, threw everything on a moving truck, and bid goodbye to America's most gorgeous city once more. As Taylor and I began our journey, I was relieved to see Los Angeles fade into the rearview mirror, leaving another chapter behind, one that remains a little blurrier than the others.

We'd met Pantera (the indisputable metal monarchs) earlier that year at an Ozzfest show in the UK, where we were asked to step in for

Korn at the last minute, a horrifying request. Don't get me wrong: I was a devoted metal fan my entire life. At heart, a back-patch-wearing, cassette-collecting, fanzine-subscribing, stage-diving lifer. But what about Ozzfest? What about the Foo Fighters? In comparison to the bludgeoning metal of the other acts, we were the rock and roll equivalent of Revenge of the Nerds. At the time, several of us even had hair ABOVE our collars, so this made no sense to me. This was possibly the greatest mismatch in history. A disaster just waiting to happen... To make matters worse, we were scheduled to follow Pantera. The ultimate heavy, tight, grooviest, badass metal band of all time. The Cro-Magnon carnage kings. HELL'S COWBOYS. "Believe me, nothing will be left once they play their final chord," I warned my manager. The stage has ended. Minds and PAs were blown. All that remained was a muddy field of smashed eardrums and melted brains. But, never one to turn down a good opportunity, we agreed and set our sights on Milton Keynes.

The National Bowl in Milton Keynes has seen its fair share of rock and roll spectacles. The stadium had held decades of big events inside its natural settings (supposedly a former clay pit for brick manufacture), from Michael Jackson to Metallica, Queen to Green Day, Status Quo to the Prodigy. It was the ideal venue for a gorgeous, bright Saturday of dread, with a capacity of 65 thousand and only fifty miles northwest of London. And the lineup was insanely strong. Sabbath, Slayer, Soulfly, and... uh... us. The day was set to be a massive metal clash of epic proportions. As I approached the backstage area, I glanced out the tour bus window, hoping to catch a glimpse of any of my heroes. Araya, Tom! Ian Scott! Iommi, Tony! Cavalera, Max! They were out and about like the rest of us. And in broad daylight, no less! I had always thought (hoped) that these dark beings only appeared at night after hanging upside down in their mausoleums like bats, nocturnal creatures denying the sun and waiting to scare us all with their wicked chants beneath a full moon. To my chagrin, I believe I noticed a handful of them wearing shorts and holding soda pops, but whatever. Metal exists. I hid in our dressing room for fear of being eaten alive. Plus, I couldn't bear walking up to the stage and getting a horrified sight of our certain fate in that undulating mosh pit of leather and spikes. I sat uncomfortably perusing our old catalogue for anything without the word "love" or a George Harrison-style slide guitar solo, trying to invent a set list that was a little more Motörhead, a little less 10cc. More than everything, I wanted to impress my hard rock heroes, hoping that they would see that I, too, was a metalhead at heart.

Finally getting up the nerve to leave my sweaty porta-cabin, I stepped to the side of the stage and witnessed Pantera's most amazing, most brutal, and most disgusting exhibition of power known to man. They were completely trashing the stage, just as I had predicted. The master, the legend, Vinnie Paul, pounding the everliving shit out of his thunderous mountain of drums. Phil Anselmo screamed horrible murder like a guy possessed by every bad spirit in every exorcism film ever created. Rex Brown stalked the stage, his bass wielded like a giant fire aiming at the audience. And Dimebag Darrell... God's gift to guitar, taking the stage with such ease, swagger, and cool that jaws were dragging in the July dirt. It was a volume called Valhalla. I noticed a crazed, shirtless fan shattering bottles and moshing alone, singing along to every word as if his life depended on it at one point. THIS was a die-hard Pantera fan. Not unlike the other 64,999 people in the bowl, mind you, but this guy was going completely insane just within a few feet of the drum set. He then knelt down to the drums to reposition a cymbal stand that had slipped as a result of Vinnie Paul's brutal banging. How odd, I thought. This insane, shirtless, slam-dancing fan turned out to be Vinnie's drum tech, Kat. Let me tell you, I've never seen anything so badass in all my years of touring. There was no road crew. It was a group of thugs. And this was no band. It was a freaking natural force.

I forgot we were even on the bill that day for a moment. I was so engrossed in the music that I forgot I had to follow this historic performance with my own kind of post-grunge alternative rock (cue fingers shoving down my throat). To find this feeling, some individuals meditate, some go to church, and still others kiss small frogs in the desert. Pantera was all I needed that day. Unfortunately, that happy mood vanished the moment they ended and the crowd screamed angrily. We cooked.

I don't remember much about our set (sometimes horrific memories are suppressed and pushed down to the darkest depths of your brain, only to be awakened by years of tough therapy), but I do remember a few guys from the other bands watching us while we were playing. That, at the very least, made me feel less like a fish out of water. When I saw these heavy metal heroes singing along to our songs word for word, I felt validated. Thankfully, we made it through the show without being pelted with bottles of urine, so I considered it a huge success. That yelling, angry throng wasn't as ferocious as it had been, but we got it back to our small room without losing any limbs. Phew.

Following that, we had the privilege of meeting and hanging out with Pantera, and anyone who has had the opportunity to hang out with Pantera knows that it is not for the faint of heart. To begin with, there has never been a band more open, hospitable, and down-to-earth as Pantera. It didn't matter who you were, what you did, or where you came from; they'd welcome you in, hand you a beer and a shot, and make you laugh harder than you'd ever laughed before. We got along great, and as we said our inebriated goodbyes, Vinnie handed me a business card. "Dude, next time you're in Dallas, you gotta come by the Clubhouse." When I looked at the card, I was surprised (but not surprised) to see that they had THEIR OWN STRIP CLUB. Some rock stars own pricey automobiles. Some people have castles. Some even have unusual animals. A fucking strip club, on the other hand? That is incredible. That's equivalent to me owning a Starbucks. Danger. Months later, while Taylor and I were preparing our journey back to Virginia with our old, dog-eared road atlas, we realised that this was our big chance to observe Pantera's wild world firsthand, so we planned the entire trip around visiting the Clubhouse. It was finally time. We stopped at a petrol station in Barstow on our first day of driving to empty our bladders and fill up with gas. Windows down, speakers distorted from blaring classic rock at 90 mph, just two best friend/drummer males speeding down the interstate carefree. We were all sunglasses and hair, cigarettes hanging from wide smiles, risking our lives by air drumming while flying by eighteen-wheelers that were blowing like sails in the desert wind. From my Flavor Flav-sized cell phone, I contacted and texted our Texan buddies, saying, "Be ready, we're on our way."

I slapped my back pocket as I approached the counter at a roadside motel in Phoenix, as I always did before pulling out my favourite green Velcro-and-vinyl wallet (Fort Knox, as it was humorously referred to). But it didn't produce the typical thump this time. My wallet was completely empty. My wallet had vanished. It had to be in the truck. I examined the cup holders. The console in the middle. Below the chairs. This is the glove compartment. Nothing. Zilch. Gone. We'd only stopped once that day, at a gas station in Barstow... FUCK. What more could I have done? That was 372.9 miles in the other direction! Everything I owned was stored in that old wallet. Dimebag Darrell guitar pick, licence, credit cards, cigarette money... I was completely screwed. Taylor, thankfully, saved the day and reserved our hotel, while I called my accountant in Seattle and made plans to ship some new cards to our next roadside motel. We soldiered on, however. Nothing, and I mean NOTHING, could keep us from reaching the Clubhouse...

Anyone who is familiar with American geography understands that Dallas is not necessarily "on the way" from Los Angeles to Virginia. No. If you're taking I-40 across, it's a real two-hundred-mile detour. But the heart wants what the heart wants, so what's a couple hundred miles compared to the stories we'd have to tell when I returned to my old Springfield neighbourhood friends? Stories to make David Lee Roth's toes curl... tales of mischief to make Keith Richards hide his ears in disgust... indeed, even Lemmy might crack a smile... We were authorised for takeoff after dinner with some of Taylor's relatives at a genuine Texas roadside eatery. We jumped in the Tahoe and drove the short distance to the Clubhouse outside of town. Actually, we may have flown there on a rainbow wave of cotton candy unicorn glitter, but it could just be my romantic revisionism at work (it happens from time to time). Whatever the case, it was happening. Months of waking up every day, counting down the minutes until we walked into Pantera's palace, surrounded by the aroma of Coors Light and peach body wash, DJ blasting old-school Scorpions, to find a booth full of Pantera just waiting to greet us with a big, Pearl Jam-style high five. I had the entire scenario memorised. It was like the kitchen scene from Goodfellas on acid. And it was going to fall.

"ID, please."

The doorman stood there, ready to go, with his glow-in-the-dark hand stamp, waiting for me to perform that old familiar smack on the back pocket that everyone does before whipping out their own trusty Fort Knox. I gazed at Taylor, my eyes wide with surprise. He mirrored my terrified expression. My cheeks turned red, tears welled up in my eyes, and I began to quiver in dread. "B-B-B-B-B-B-B-Barstow... I lost my wallet in Barstow, sir," I mumbled. Silence. Then, more than the grim reaper himself, the words I dreaded burst from the doorman's sneer: "Sorry, bud. We can't let you in without identification." Taylor interjected, "But, but, but... we're friends with Pantera!" "Everyone's friends with Pantera," the man hissed, looking up with icy, dead eyes. Sorry."

And that was the end of it. Three days, fourteen hundred miles, and a dream trampled out in the parking lot of an industrial complex outside of Dallas like a filthy old Parliament Light. There was no sugar coating here; it fucked up my soul. We gently climbed back into the Tahoe, heads down, hearts broken, completely devastated, after a few more unanswered calls from the Flavor Flav phone and a few more cigarettes in the parking lot. Pantera will not be hanging out with us. Taylor would never let me forget what happened.

THEN I WAS ON MY WAY HOME AGAIN.

Ten years later, in Oxnard, California, I was buying sunglasses with my infant daughter Violet at a local surf shop near the bay, and as we approached the cash register, the nice girl behind the counter welcomed me with a greeting and proceeded to ring up my purchase. "Are you Dave Grohl?" she questioned, looking up after a little pause. "Yes," I replied, smiling. "Did you lose your wallet in Barstow in 1998?" she said, squinting.

No. Fucking. Way.

"YES!!!!!!!!!!" I responded in awe. "That was my parents' gas station," she chuckled. They've still got your wallet, guy."

I gave up trying to comprehend fate and destiny a long time ago, but it appears that stupid luck is my specialty. Surprisingly, my wallet was returned to me not long after that, entirely undamaged, and still loaded with wonderful mementos from that glorious period in my life, when I was young, free, and ready to start again. My previous driver's licence was also inside. When we arrived in Virginia a week later, my ears ringing from days of classic rock and in desperate need of long showers, I walked into my new house and immediately felt at home, just blocks from my father's old apartment, which I used to walk to every Tuesday and Thursday after Catholic school, and a short drive from my mother's. This was a homecoming to the area that shaped me, and unlike in Seattle or Los Angeles, I felt at home. I was no longer a wanderer crashing on a stranger's sofa or passing through; I had returned to my forever home. It was almost as if I had never left, made even more so by the fact that I was now living with my oldest buddy, Jimmy Swanson.

Since sixth grade, Jimmy and I had been inseparable. We marched through life like Siamese twins, every formative experience mirroring in a parallel path. We explored everything together, like brothers, and we didn't see each other every day. Jimmy was a year my senior, tall with a Scandinavian physique, his blue eyes concealed behind his nicely feathered dirty blond hair, which he kept in check with a plastic comb he kept in his back pocket. A true rocker. A lifelong outcast. He was the epitome of heavy metal parking-lot cool, minus the irony. He was the genuine article. I followed Jimmy wherever he went because I wanted to be just like him. He and I were never cut out to be valedictorian homecoming kings, so we created our own little world as outcasts, huddled in front of the boombox in his bedroom, discovering metal, punk rock, and weed together, becoming so close that we didn't need words to communicate, instead relying on our own ESP. This was especially significant because Jimmy had a severe stutter that hampered him socially throughout his life, thus he retained a small group of pals. He was a knight in weathered denim, always kind and polite, and he was as much my home as the house I grew up in. So, since we'd shared everything our entire lives, it seemed only natural that I'd share this new house with him as well. Though we'd never lost touch (Jimmy had toured with both Nirvana and the Foo Fighters over the years), it had been a long time since we could say, "Hey, man, I'll be over in five minutes...," and spend the day together in our little world, so returning to him felt like a return to myself, a much needed reunion. With no prior expertise in establishing a recording studio, I began researching equipment, design, and materials, as well as reaching out to a few of my amazing engineer and producer pals for guidance on how to turn my crappy little basement into the next

Abbey Road. One of them was Adam Kasper, a terrific producer and Seattle buddy with whom I had previously collaborated, most memorably on Nirvana's final session in January 1994. Adam had a wicked sense of humour and a very relaxed, analog recording style, so he seemed like the perfect guy to not just assist create a cheap basement studio but also produce our next record. The Colour and the Shape, produced by Gil Norton, the guy behind the Pixies' classic singles, was a long, laborious, hyper-technical affair that took its toll on the band during those trying months in the woods outside of Seattle. Gil was a known taskmaster, and his rigorous attention to detail paid off in the end, but only after thirty to forty takes of each song. We swore we'd never go through that ordeal again, so the prospect of returning to Virginia and constructing a basic little studio in a house with Adam Kasper sounded much more tempting. We only needed one 24-track machine, one vintage mixing console, a few microphones, and a few compressors, and we started looking for the hardware as we transformed my basement into a soundproofed chamber of rock. My mother would frequently stop by to check on the progress, and I would take her on a tour from room to room, doing my best to explain the science behind the precise acoustic design required to build a studio (something I knew nothing about, but because I'm a seasoned bullshit artist, she bought it hook, line, and sinker). I suppose Mom was mostly relieved to be able to visit me anytime she wanted after years away.

On one of her weekly inspections, we heard the sound of a tiny kitten meowing for help from somewhere among the rubble heaps spread throughout the room. We were startled and began hurriedly exploring every area of the studio for it, but it appeared to be moving. "It's right over here!" I said, and my mother dashed to my side of the studio. Silence. "No, it's over here!" said my mother, and I dashed to her side of the room. Again, silence. We went back and forth for a few minutes, perplexed by the kitten's ability to toss its little voice in every direction. We stood completely still, trying not to scare it away. I gently said to my mother, "Maybe it's inside a wall," and then crawled across the unclean floor on my knees, putting my ear to the freshly painted drywall, hoping to find this helpless animal. My mother approached me cautiously, and I heard a faint meow. "Shhhh!" I exclaimed. She took another step forward. Meow. It was getting closer, I thought. My mother, who was standing just next me, leaned in to listen and... meow. "Hey, Mom... will you shift your weight on your right foot for a second?" I asked, looking down at my mother's footwear.

Meow.

The cat we'd been chasing around the studio for 45 minutes happened to be my mother's right sandal, which was "meowing" every time she took a step. We both collapsed on the floor, scarcely able to breathe, grateful that no one else was present to watch the two of us in this most absurd situation, which we still laugh about to this day.

Spring, my favourite season in Virginia, arrived with the completion of the studio. After months of cold, dead leaves, and barren trees, the sun came out, and nature was soon in full bloom, a rebirth that matched somewhat poetically with our newfound independence as a band, and we opened all the windows to welcome the new chapter in. What I had envisaged as a cutting-edge recording studio turned out to be a very basic, no-frills setup, with packing foam, pillows, and sleeping bags strewn about for sound treatment. This was the meaning of DIY to me, an idea I had acquired and attempted to follow since my days in the punk music scene in Washington, DC, when we all did everything ourselves, from scheduling shows to founding our own record labels to releasing our modest records on vinyl. When you accomplished things yourself, the prize was usually much sweeter. And here we were, years later, figuring things out as we went along, step by step, in the most unsophisticated and blissfully innocent manner, but most importantly, we were hidden away from any industry expectations, left to find who we truly were as a band.

Our daily regimen was straightforward. Since the band had moved in with Jimmy and me, my days had always started with some housework: removing overflowing ashtrays, disposing of heated, half-empty Coors Light cans, and cleaning the hardwood floors like a haggard maid from hell in soiled sweatpants. Each member would emerge one by one, staring at the coffee pot like a crackhead waiting for the pipe as it slowly brewed. Taylor would grumble about the "ducks" (crows) outside his window, and we'd slowly awaken, planning our days around the kitchen table. Perhaps a few rounds of hoops in the driveway before lunch, followed by a review of the previous night's recordings in the basement. We'd work all day, end with a few drinks and a barbecue out back while the fireflies danced around the grill, and then pass out in the living room while Jimmy took bong hit after bong hit from his favourite recliner. This was our daily routine, and it was precisely because we were so comfortable that these recordings seem the most natural-sounding in our whole collection. When combined with the limitations imposed by the studio's limited technological capability, it resulted in a simple, raw, and honest recording. Not to mention that I was infatuated with AM Gold music at the time (soft rock favourites from the 1970s), possibly because it reminded me of growing up listening to the radio while I drove the same streets that I had returned to. Those lush, melancholic melodies from Andrew Gold, Gerry Rafferty, Peter Frampton, Helen Reddy, and Phoebe Snow were making their way into our new compositions. At the time, popular rock music had shifted its focus to a new genre, nu metal, which I like but wanted to be the polar opposite of, so I purposefully proceeded in the opposite way. Most nu metal songs lacked melody, and it was my love of melody (influenced by the Beatles from a young age) that prompted me to compose from a much gentler place. That, combined with the tremendous sense of regeneration brought on by the Virginia spring, gave rise to songs like "Ain't It the Life," "Learn to Fly," "Aurora," and "Generator," all fantastic instances of a guy finally at ease in his surroundings, no longer wandering but somewhere he belonged. We had completed what I still consider to be our best album, There Is Nothing Left to Lose, by the end of our sessions in June.

And we gave our new studio, which would serve us well for years to come, a name: Studio 606.

A year and a half later, as I stood at the Grammys podium to accept the Best Rock Album award, I looked out at the audience of musicians and industry players, all dripping in diamonds and dressed in the latest fashion, and felt a huge sense of pride that we had created this all on our own, away from the glitter and shiny lights of Hollywood, making our very first Grammy even sweeter. If there was ever a time when I believed we deserved a trophy, it was then. We had not only captured the sound of regeneration and renewal brought on by the majestic Virginia spring from our little ramshackle basement studio buried in the woods I had once climbed as a child, but we had also found a return to who we once were. Years of overcoming adversity after adversity, death, divorce, and a revolving door of band members, I had persisted and emerged stronger, but not yet ready to buy the farm. There was still plenty of work to be done. And with this new trophy, which symbolised our renewed attitude, one thing was clear: WE DID NOT HAVE TO DO THIS ANYMORE. WE WANTED TO DO THIS INSTANTLY.

CHAPTER 9
THIS IS WHAT I WANTED

"Mom . . . we're having a girl."

My mother's voice cracked as she started crying. "Oh, David...," she mumbled. "Oh my goodness . . ." There was a long gap as she put down the phone to wipe the tears of pride from her cheeks, and as I stood in my backyard trying to understand what I had just spoken, it hit me. I was expecting a daughter. My mother was ecstatic. I was taken aback. I'd always known I'd be a father someday, but I imagined it would be after this life of touring and travelling was finished. "You know this isn't going to last, right?" my father had asked years earlier. I had assumed that the music would simply stop and that I would be able to establish a new life of domestic anonymity. I've seen others struggle to raise a family while travelling (preach, Steve Perry!) However, because of my traditional upbringing, I thought that idea to be too shaky and lacking in stability. I always got the shivers when I saw a Pack 'n Play next to a table full of alcohol and Jägermeister. I didn't know these two cultures could coexist until the Foo Fighters were invited to perform at Neil Young's Bridge School Benefit in 2000. The Bridge School Benefit was an annual weekend-long concert organised by Neil and Pegi Young to raise funds for the Bridge School, a nonprofit organisation Pegi founded to find a home for their son Ben, who has cerebral palsy, and other children with severe speech and physical impairments to help them with language and communication needs. Each year, the performance was hosted at the Shoreline Amphitheatre just outside of San Francisco, with fantastic lineups like Springsteen, Dylan, McCartney, Petty, the Beach Boys, Pearl Jam, and Metallica (to mention a few). These gatherings raised millions of dollars, and the feeling of love and joy was unlike anything I had ever experienced. Every single person in the room was there for the kids, and I was persuaded that the community energy of so much positivity in one area had its own healing power.

The weekend always started with a BBQ at Neil's house on Broken Arrow Ranch, a magnificent, rustic 140-acre paradise in Redwood City that he bought in 1970 and where he would invite all of the performers for supper the night before the show. I imagined a formally catered celebration, tables lined with rock and roll royalty rattling their gleaming cutlery, laps lined with linen napkins, while they told mythical folklore of yesteryear, as we drove down the winding mountain roads deep in the redwoods toward his home. That could not be farther from the truth. When we got at the gate, there was a hand-painted sign hanging from the decaying fence that screamed DON'T SPOOK THE HORSE, and after entering the property, it was another ten-minute drive through twisting hills before we spotted the modest house, lit up like a Christmas tree in the distance. It appeared to be the creation of a crazed survivalist with a passion for tree houses, replete with a bellower and a large tent in the yard, and was part Harry Potter, part Swiss Family Robinson. You strolled right in, no valet parking, no reception. Pegi, who had been cutting vegetables by the sink, greeted me with a hearty hug as I entered the kitchen. She provided me with a mudroom coat in case it was cold outside, but cautioned me to "check the pockets for mice." David Crosby was seated in front of the fireplace. Brian Wilson was lost and searching for his wife. Tom Petty's band was on the porch, and Neil's children were among us. This was not at all a formal rock and roll event. This was a residence. This was a household. THIS IS WHAT I DESIRED, AND NOW I SEE HOW IT IS POSSIBLE.

As my mother regained her composure after learning she would have a granddaughter, I explained to her that, while I'd always known I'd be a father eventually, I'd never anticipated having a female. I'm not a cigar-chomping,NASCAR-watching,Sunday-afternoon-armchair-quarterback type, but what could I possibly offer a daughter? How does she tune a kick drum and organise her Slayer bootlegs? I was at a loss for words. And then, as she always did, my mother shared some of her hard-won wisdom, which has since proven to be one of life's most unmistakable truths: "The relationship between a father and daughter can be one of the most special relationships in any girl's life." She knew this because of her father, a military man of charm and wit who everyone adored before his untimely death when she was in her thirties. I never got the chance to meet him, but from what I've heard, he was a decent man with a unique connection to my mother. I was marginally reassured, despite the fact that I was still afraid. It could be fun to catalogue Slayer bootlegs together. Jordyn and I proceeded to prepare for the new baby as the months passed, preparing her room, purchasing for all the required things, and eventually settling on the name Violet (after my mother's mother, Violet Hanlon). I was given a library of books to read on topics ranging from sleep training (which is a farce because they eventually sleep-train you, making it impossible for you to sleep past six a.m. for the rest of your life) to swaddling (I'm bad enough at rolling joints; how could I successfully roll a child?) to diaper changing (something I may hold a land speed record in by this point). I was getting a crash course in parenting, or at the very least the logistics of it.

"Hey, you wanna write songs with John Fogerty?" my manager said one day near the end of Jordyn's pregnancy. The answer, as it would be for any rock and roll fan who grew up in the 1970s, was an enthusiastic "Duh." I was advised to meet John at his property in the hills a few days later for a songwriting session. When he opened the door to his home studio, I was met by the icon himself, dressed precisely how you'd expect him to be: flannel shirt, jeans, and work boots. We talked for a long time, sharing jokes and telling horror stories from our turbulent pasts, and when the guitars were finally brought out, he began singing lyrics off the top of his head based on our private conversation. His signature voice, raw and soulful, was directly in front of my face, but it sounded so loud it seemed like it was coming straight from a stadium PA system. It was a beautiful moment that reminded me why he is regarded as an American treasure: he is genuine.

We walked down to his kitchen for bowls of minestrone and SunChips (if John Fogerty hadn't been sitting there, I'd have sworn I was home sick from school), but I kept an eye on the clock, knowing that I only had until four thirty to leave. "Welp... wanna jam a little more?" he asked after lunch. But I had to disappoint him by telling him that I couldn't stay because I had an appointment with my pregnant wife. "Where are you going'?" he inquired. "Breast-feeding class," I responded with a tinge of discomfort in my voice, to which he smiled and said, "Can I come?"

Night after night, despite how strange it may appear to some, I would speak to Violet in the womb because I was looking forward to the day when I could hold her in my arms instead of just talking to my wife's pajamas like a fucking lunatic. When the big day arrived, I was nervously packing the car to drive to the hospital when I noticed a huge rainbow overhead, which happens maybe once every thousand years in Los Angeles. I was immediately at ease. Yes, it sounds sickly romantic, but it's true, and I took it as a sign.

After a long and tough labour, Violet was delivered to the tune of the Beatles in the backdrop, and she arrived screaming with a predefined vocal capability that made the Foo Fighters sound like the Carpenters. Once she was cleaned up and put under the little Arby's heat-lamp bed, I put my face near hers, peered into her enormous blue eyes, and said, "Hey, Violet, it's Dad." She suddenly stopped screaming and her eyes locked with mine. She recognized my voice. We stared at each other in stillness, our first introduction, and I smiled and talked to her as if I had known her my whole life. I am delighted to say that, still to this day, when we lock eyes it's the same emotion.

This was a love I had never experienced before. There is an innate insecurity that comes along with being a successful singer that makes you question love. Do they adore me? Or do they love "it"? You are showered with superficial love and affection on a regular basis, giving you something similar to a sugar high, but your heart falls as the thrill goes down. Is it possible for someone to view a musician without the instrument being a part of their identity? Or is that a part of the identity that the other loves? Regardless, it's a dangerous and slippery slope to question love, but one thing is for certain: there is nothing purer than the unconditional love between a parent and their child.

Once the delivery was over and we were led to our hospital room for the night, Jordyn was famished, so I went down to the cafeteria to find her something to eat. I scoured for something that she might actually be able to stomach but retreated back to our room empty-handed, opting to perhaps order from the Jerry's Deli across the street. I walked across the hall to the nurse station, where there was one nurse on duty, a large woman with Hulk Hogan's build who barked at me in a thick eastern European accent, "CAN I HELP YOU?" "Yes . . . um, can you tell me if Jerry's Deli delivers here?" She stared at me with her ice-cold eyes and growled, "I AM NOT AT LIBERTY TO DISCLOSE ANY INFORMATION ABOUT WHO IS DELIVERED HERE." I smiled, realising that she'd misunderstood my question, and said, "Hahaha . . . no . . . does JERRY'S DELI deliver here?" Looking like she was about to leap over her computer and strangle me with her giant, professional-wrestling hands, she raised her volume and repeated, "I TOLD YOU! I AM NOT AT LIBERTY TO DISCLOSE ANY INFORMATION ABOUT WHO IS DELIVERED HERE!!!" I scurried away in fear, walked across the street, and ordered a sandwich for Jordyn while standing next to Jennifer Lopez.

Another night in Los Angeles.

My mother was right, being a father to a daughter was indeed the most special relationship of my life. I was soon well versed in the art of a smudgeless pedicure, how to tie the perfect ponytail, and how to identify every Disney princess just by the colour of her dress. This was easy, I thought.

THEN CAME THE HARD PART: BALANCING THE NEW LIFE WITH THE OLD.

I remember the first time I had to leave Violet behind for a tour. I stood above her crib as she slept, and I began to cry. How could I possibly leave this little miracle behind? I had to tear myself away, and so began a lifetime of leaving half of my heart at home. At this point, all of the band members were procreating like rabbits, and our tour itineraries were now dictated by people who couldn't even chew solid food yet, so what had been six-week tours were whittled down to two weeks at the most. As much as touring in a rock band is hands-down the best fucking job on earth, it can be exhausting, but the minute you set foot back in your house after a few weeks away, you are handed a screaming baby and are officially on daddy duty 24/7. This, of course, is partly to relieve your wife of the maternal duties that she was overwhelmed with from sunrise to sunset while you were out shotgunning beers with your best friends (cue slight resentment) but more so because you feel the need to overcompensate for your absence. You are forever haunted by the fear that the time away from your child will leave them with lifelong psychological repercussions, so when you're home, you are HOME. Tour, home, tour, home, tour, home . . . after a few years of that, you begin to find the balance, and you realise that the two worlds CAN coexist. So why not do it again?

This time, it'll be a boy, I thought.

Having already mastered the role of "dad who knows every word to every Little Mermaid song," I was now ready to try my hand at raising a son. And I already had the name picked out: Harper Bonebrake Grohl, named after my father's uncle, Harper Bonebrake (we called him Uncle Buzz).

The Bonebrake family tree can be traced all the way back to Johann Christian Beinbrech, who was baptised in Switzerland on February 9, 1642, eventually immigrating to Germany and fathering eleven children. It was his grandson Daniel Beinbrech who bravely travelled to America by ship and settled in a wilderness called Pigeon Hills around York, Pennsylvania, in September 1762.

Numerous offspring and various spellings followed (Pinebreck, Bonbright) until the most awesome "Bonebrake" moniker was landed on with Daniel's son Peter, who was an American Revolutionary soldier who had nine children of his own. By 1768, the name was set in stone and carried all the way to the birth of my uncle Buzz and my grandmother Ruth Viola Bonebrake in 1909, to their parents Harper and Emma. In turn, my father was named James Harper Grohl, so in keeping with tradition, I decided to name my son Harper as well. (We proudly have a Civil War Congressional Medal of Honor recipient, Henry G. Bonebrake, and the drummer of Los Angeles punk legends X, D. J. Bonebrake, in the family tree as well.)

"Mom . . . we're having another girl."

To be clear, I truly never had any gender preference, but I did really want to name a child Harper Bonebrake Grohl. So, we named her Harper (never got the Bonebrake past the goalie) and she was born only two days after Violet's third birthday. The feeling of overwhelming paternal love was renewed, and now I had two daughters to fawn over, Violet walking and talking at a level far beyond her age, and Harper (my spitting image) cooing in my lap, never without a smile. This was a residence. This was a household. This is what I wanted. As I watched every step of their development, it was hard not to think about my parents doing the same. I have very few memories of these years in my life, most of them with my mother, who showered me with unconditional love, and not so much with my father. My parents divorced when I was only six years old, leaving me to be raised by my mother, and I had a hard time grasping this separation now as a father myself. How could he not want to spend every waking minute bouncing me on his lap, pushing me on the swing, or reading me stories every night before bed? Was it that he didn't want to? Or that he didn't know how? Perhaps this was the crux of my fear of being an absent parent, my overcompensation every time I returned home after being away. As lucky as I was to be raised by my amazing mother, I was seeing how the broken relationship with my father and his absence in my childhood had some lifelong psychological repercussions, and that I was desperate to not create those for my own children. We began to travel the world with our daughters, and I no longer felt strange about a backstage full of children (though they were in their own dressing room so they wouldn't be playing next to the beer and Jägermeister), because no matter where on the planet we were, if we were together, it was home. The life that my father warned would never last had blossomed into what I had witnessed that night at Neil Young's house: music and family intertwined. It was possible after all.

CHAPTER 10
DOWN UNDER DUI

"Asseyez-vous, s'il vous plaît . . ."

Confused, I asked my French-speaking girlfriend, who was serving as interpreter, for help, and she answered, "She wants you to sit down." I nodded and slid into the chair across from the older woman, nervously smiling as she scrutinised my every move. I had reason to be conflicted about this unexpected meeting. I'd never visited a psychic before.

It was January 2000, and the Foo Fighters were in Australia for the Big Day Out, Australia's largest annual tour, which began in 1992 with a Sydney-only show featuring Nirvana and the Violent Femmes, and eventually grew to a massive three-week, six-city extravaganza hosting up to a hundred bands each year. It was the top of any touring band's itinerary, set in the blistering heat of the magnificent Aussie summer, given the casual pace of six gigs in three weeks, making it more of a vacation in the sun than the typical hard tempo we were all used to. We dubbed it "The Big Day Off," and we made the most of every opportunity offstage. My fiancée had flown down from the United States for a quick vacation, and she had her heart set on seeing a well-known French psychic who resided in an apartment complex outside of Sydney. She had apparently visited her before on another tour to Australia with her own band years ago, and this person was the real deal, according to those familiar with the phenomenon. Over the years, our old friend/promoter Stephen Pavlovic had brought other mystical musicians to her, all of whom had returned home with wonderful assessments of her perceptive abilities. I had never seen a legitimate psychic for the simple reason that I had no interest in them. With the exception of one ridiculous card reading in a New Orleans souvenir shop during Nirvana's zenith of glory, where I was told by a woman with a bone in her nose, "Don't give up, someday you'll make it!" I had managed to avoid any staged psychic reflection. I didn't doubt that some people have the ability to read your mind and see into the future; I just didn't want to know what they saw. In some ways, I preferred to keep the future a mystery for fear of changing it by following someone else's incorrect forecast. I believed that life should take its natural course, a journey without a map to refer to if you get lost.

This woman's method was simple: bring a photograph of yourself, any one, and she would silently scrutinise it while tracing her fingers down your figure, obtaining some kind of supernatural knowledge with her touch before offering her psychic assessment. Remember, this was not an appointment I had booked for myself, but for my girlfriend, who had prepared for this meeting by bringing her own portfolio of photographs, one of which included one of myself. We were only chaperoning/chauffeuring her to this woman's place for the session, so we dashed off to get a coffee while they made contact with the other side. When we returned, my girlfriend was fatigued from her reading, and the psychic swiftly switched her attention to me, as I had obviously been a difficult topic of conversation while we were away. Because she spoke very little English and required translation, my girlfriend and I had an unpleasant relationship as I relied on her (a Montreal local) to explain the psychic's most private disclosures, no matter how uncomfortable they were for her to hear. After viewing my photos for a few minutes, the psychic reached out and carefully touched my hands, surveying the lines and calluses from years of torture.

"You have a lot of energy..." she replied.

When I turned to my partner for help, she said, "She says you have a lot of energy."

Ah! She's getting off to a wonderful start! "Yes, I'm kind of hyperactive," I said in English, hoping she'd understand, which she did with a little help from my partner.

"Non, tu as beaucoup d'énergie psychique..."

I didn't need a translator for this. She was claiming that I possessed psychic energy. My face brightened up with delight. This was becoming interesting.

"Tes mains brillent... elles ont une aura... c'est bleue... très puissante..."

My hands, according to my new clairvoyant best buddy, shone with a bright blue aura. Whether I believed her or not, I was ecstatic, if not pleased, by her telepathic declaration. How could I have missed this? I pondered. I could have used my powerful blue aura all along! Then she raised her head and inquired if I had seen any ghosts. This was a challenging question to answer. Had I ever been visited by a traditional floating apparition who had crossed over from the other side to retake its former land in a cliché haunting? No. Had I been witness to a series of unexplained incidents in which I thought I was in the presence of something neither alive nor dead? Yes.

At the height of Nirvana's fame, I was still living in a small room with only a dresser, a nightstand, and a futon mattress on the floor, because the band grew so quickly that I didn't have time to adjust to my new life as a rock star. In actuality, I had no urge to go out and spend my growing bank account since I was completely content with the way things were. I never had much, thus I never required much, and this living situation felt very natural to me. But, above all, it was enjoyable. On a rainy afternoon, sitting around watching MTV and eating Totino's Party Pizzas with my buddies was my concept of "making it," so why alter anything?

My father (my default financial counsel) eventually convinced me that it was time to invest in a house of my own in Seattle for the purpose of equity (and to keep me from spending all of my money on Slim Jims and cigarettes), so he travelled out and we began our search together. We spent a few days browsing through houses, seeking for the perfect fit, after a local real estate agent compiled various listings around town. Most were either too old, too strange, or too far away from amenities, but one struck out: a newly built home in Richmond Beach, a northern Seattle suburb. It was situated among dense pines at the end of a dead-end street, just blocks from the magnificent Puget Sound, a pretty modest and unassuming house at first appearance. However, upon entering, you were greeted by an architectural masterpiece. Multiple levels of landings and rooms framed in beautiful wood, all flooded with natural light from skylights placed into the great ceilings and massive windows overlooking the dense forest outside. Because the house was built on top of a hill, it appeared to be only one level from the driveway, but the back of the house was carefully built down the terraced property behind, with decks and landings facing the enormous evergreens out back. It was difficult to picture living alone in such a large space, but

I was pulled to its warmth and design, swiftly grabbing it up and moving my dresser, nightstand, and futon in with ease.

The first night at the house, I sat on my old futon with my back against the bedroom wall, viewing my new television (real rock & roll excess!). The rain was falling in sheets, and I was getting a little anxious about being alone in this vast mansion, when the house rocked with a huge BANG! It wasn't lightning or thunder, nor was it an explosion from outside. This sounded like an 18-wheeler had crashed into the wall against which I was propped up, jolting my body forward as if I'd been rear-ended. I instantly pressed the mute button on the remote and sat perfectly still, frozen with horror. I eventually had the nerve to leave my bedroom and peer down from the little landing into the vacant living room, examining the dark space for any moving shadows or evidence of an intruder. I had goosebumps all over my body from terror as I tiptoed silently from one room to the next, expecting to find proof of a break-in, but there was none. When I got back to bed, I turned off the TV and slept with one eye open for the rest of the night. She then inquired as to whether I had seen any UFOs. This was certainly something I was interested in. After all, I named my band the Foo Fighters after the World War II slang term for unidentified flying objects; our record label imprint is called Roswell Records after the 1947 UFO crash in Roswell, New Mexico; and my publishing company is called MJ Twelve Music, which is a reference to Harry S. Truman's alleged secret committee of scientists, military leaders, and government officials assembled to recover and investigate alien spacecraft. So I was well-versed in the world of UFO conspiracies, despite the fact that I had never seen one myself.

"No," I replied. "But I dream about them quite often."

She looked me in the eyes and replied, "Ce ne sont pas des rêves."

I ASKED MY FRIEND FOR TRANSLATION, AND SHE SAID, "THOSE ARE NOT DREAMS."

I immediately remembered the innumerable intense dreams I'd had as a child about being visited by extraterrestrials, which I can still remember vividly to this day. I used to imagine myself soaring through my neighbourhood, peering down at the rows of tiny dwellings below from the window of a small craft, silently hovering and blasting through the air at incredible speeds with ease, invisible to the human sight. In one, I was lying in my front yard's moist grass, staring up at the night sky full of stars, urgently hoping to conjure a UFO to transport me to another universe. As I peered into space, I realised I was looking back at my reflection in the grass, reflected by the smooth metal underbelly of a saucer-shaped ship flying barely metres above my head. And suddenly I awoke. But there is one dream that I will never forget, a dream so powerful and deeply involved that I can't get it out of my head. It was a lovely early evening in a southern European beach town, and the sky was a wonderful shade of cerulean blue in the twilight hour between sunset and full night. I was wandering down a grassy knoll, enjoying the nice summer air while looking down at the harbour below, which was bustling with cafés and couples strolling hand in hand along the promenade. The stars were just visible, brightening with each passing instant as the sun set behind the water, when the sky burst in a blinding light, sending me to the ground. I looked up and saw thousands of UFOs darting across the sky, all different sizes, shapes, and colours, and I sat there in awe, taking in this incredible event while looking around at the incredulous faces of thousands of others doing the same thing. Time had stopped. Through some type of telepathy, a thunderous voice thundered into my head. "THE EVOLUTION OF MAN," the voice said as animated graphics were projected into the sky, explaining how beings from a faraway corner of the universe aided our species' evolution. On the left side of the sky, Leonardo da Vinci's drawing Vitruvian Man was projected, and on the right, a map of the world with all of our borders and territories redrawn, while a voice announced this event to be the "DAWN OF A NEW ERA."

I awoke thinking this was more than a dream, but I carried on with my life, not allowing it to sink in enough to send me down the unfortunate and common rabbit hole from which some UFO conspiracists never recover, spending the rest of their days waiting for "full disclosure." I was moved, but the most traction this dream ever had in my life was as the basis for the Foo Fighters' video for "The Sky Is a Neighbourhood," which I directed and stars my two children Violet and Harper. It was a great dream, I thought, but it was only a dream. Until now, that is. According to the psychic, this was not my imagination, but rather reality. She then proceeded to tell me things that no one on Earth could have known after a few more favourable discoveries, including the precise dimension I'm from. This wasn't spitballing; she told me details about my life that were so specific, intimate, and spot-on that I was completely converted. I was now convinced. I was certain that this woman possessed "postcognition" (the ability to supernaturally perceive past occurrences) or an advanced sort of intuition. We concluded my session, said our goodbyes, and drove back to Sydney from her modest flat. These revelations gave me confidence, and I wondered if this was something I was born with, thinking of all the times I could have used my psychic gift to help me. Including the previous week on the Gold Coast.

The Gold Coast, a Queensland seaside town 45 minutes south of Brisbane, is Australia's equivalent to Fort Lauderdale, Florida. Beach bars brimming with blazing, neon-coloured beverages, blond-haired surfers wearing half-off wetsuits at every turn, and, yes, a Sea World theme park for the more family-oriented guests. We milked every second in this bronzed utopia for every last drop of mischief we could find, and because we were down to play the Big Day Off tour, we had plenty of time to take advantage of its juvenile trappings. Taylor and I opted to hire scooters upon arrival so that we could whizz around town throughout the day, beach to beach, for the three days leading up to our major gig at the Gold Coast Parklands, a greyhound racing track only a few miles from the city. Our hotel, the Sheraton Grand Mirage, had become one of our favourites over the years, with its seventies cocaine-white theme and gluttonous dinner buffets overlooking chlorinated pools full with displaced swans. If Scarface's Tony Montana ever had a vacation, it would certainly be here. It seemed like I was walking through a Nagel artwork while wearing flip-flops.

Fortunately, the hotel was only a few miles from the gig, a straight shot down the Smith Street Motorway, so instead of taking the overcrowded shuttle with the other bands, Taylor and I decided to drive ourselves, getting in as much Easy Rider action as we could before we had to return them and leave the next day. We set off on our short adventure without helmets (or licences), giggling at the silliness of two famous singers preparing to perform in front of 50,000 people racing down the road on tattered minibikes. It was pure comedy, just like most days back then. When we got to the venue, the local security personnel were sceptical, as if we were two sunburned American tourists who had somehow stolen backstage tickets from the authentic Foo Fighters. We were finally rescued by our tour manager, Gus, after much cajoling and unintelligible walkie-talkie communication, and sped into the backstage enclosure, weaving among the picnic tables full of bands, who pointed and laughed at us as we flew past. We were without a doubt the nerdiest, goofiest, and most obnoxious band on the lineup, except from Blink-182. I mean, there were some real heavyweights on this one—Red Hot Chili Peppers, Nine Inch Nails, and Primal Scream, to name a few—and I can safely say that none of those fellas would be caught dead going around in those dork-mobiles in broad daylight. As we were preparing for the gig, I had another insane idea: I was going to drive my scooter onstage during our performance and rev the engine like Rob Halford from Judas Priest had always done, but with a massive Harley-Davidson motorcycle, to pay tribute to the heavy metal king himself. I identified the perfect time in the act when I could come flying onstage like Evel Knievel, wind out the little 50cc engine in a cloud of smoke, and continue playing while the audience doubled over, as I sat and composed the set list over a few beers. Anything for a chuckle, I reasoned, and my plan was implemented. Everything went off without a hitch. I went back to the dressing room after the show and looked at the schedule of artists that was tacked to the wall. I spotted one of my favourite bands, the Hellacopters from Sweden, were performing on a side stage in the distance, so I grabbed a couple beers, placed Bobby Gillespie from Primal Scream on the back of my now-famous scooter, and we putted over to see them play. The Hellacopters, a hard rock bombardment of classic riffs and classic hair, never failed to put on a terrific show, and I was fortunate enough to see many of them having toured extensively with them over the years.

I saw it had begun to rain while I sat on the side of the stage headbanging and sipping my beers. It wasn't a furious tropical downpour, but it was enough to make me think it was time to head back to the hotel before it really started pouring. These scooters weren't exactly roadworthy, and even a light drizzle might turn the highway into a slick would-be tragedy, but it was just a few kilometres away, so I didn't worry too much. I gathered Taylor and pulled on my sweatshirt for the voyage back to our DeLorean-themed castle in the sand. Within a mile or so, traffic on the busy two-lane highway had come to a halt. It was late, and there was literally only one road back into town for all of the other 49,999 people who had gone to the show, so our fast ride home had turned into a virtual heavy metal parking lot. I assumed there had been an accident, and we drove at a snail's pace for what felt like an eternity. Then I noticed what was truly slowing traffic. A checkpoint for sobriety. Now I have to stop and justify why I didn't just leap off that stupid fucking scooter, park it on the side of the road, and phone Gus to come pick me up in the rain. First and foremost, it was a scooter. This contraption was roughly the size of a riding lawn mower in terms of motorization. I couldn't imagine a cop thinking twice about waving me through, most likely smirking at how ridiculous I looked attempting to keep up with traffic in my rain-soaked hoodie and camouflage shorts. Second, I didn't feel the least bit hindered by the drinking I'd done in the previous five hours. Not to brag, but it takes more than a few cans of malted beverages and a few shots of whiskey to knock me out. I honestly didn't feel drunk at all. So I was OK to go, right? Wrong.

"Blow in this, mate," the cop stated as I approached the checkpoint. Shocked, I gladly agreed as Taylor flew by, free as a bird (apparently he had abstained from booze that night, preferring to indulge in other party favours instead), blowing as hard as I could into the tiny straw at the end of the copper's little contraption. He took one look at it, then at me, and stated, in the thickest, most Crocodile Dundee Australian accent, "Step off the bike, you're over the limit..." It was impossible for me to believe. All those years of getting away with the most jackass shit you could imagine and never getting caught, and here I was in Australia being arrested for drunk driving on a fucking moped. "Pull over and take it out of gear!" that's what he said. I couldn't help but laugh. Gears? There were no gears on this thing. To get the blasted thing moving, you had to use your feet like Fred Flintstone. I set it on its kickstand, and the police requested my identification. This was now a problem. I never, ever travel with my passport because I would lose it in a hot New York minute. (Yes, I'm that guy who loses everything in his pockets every day.) Gus has always kept it for me, allowing me to touch it only when crossing a border or checking into a flight, and then requiring that I return it. All I had was the Big Day Out tour laminate around my neck, which luckily had my name, picture, and band affiliation on it, so I said, "Oh, man, my tour manager has my passport, but I do have this," and handed it over in the hopes that he would be a huge fan and let me go. MAYBE FOR ONE TIME, THIS ROCK STAR NAME-DROP WOULD WORK. NOPE.

"Musician, huh?" he asked, with a newfound confidence. I explained that we were on the Big Day Out tour and had been in his lovely city for a few days, hence the ludicrous scooter. "Ah...," he admitted. "When's the next show?" "Tomorrow in Sydney," I said, a spark of hope in my eyes. "Sorry, mate, but you're going to miss that one." I'm going to have to take you to jail." Panic ensued. I said that from where we were standing, I could practically see the hotel and that I could easily park this piece of trash and walk the rest of the way. "Sorry, mate," was all I received back. I had been fucked.

Taylor, who had made it through the checkpoint and doubled back to make sure I was okay, pulled up next to us and asked, "Dude, what's going on???" I informed him that I was on my way to jail and that he should hurry back to the hotel and have Gus prepare my bail. Taylor sped away ("sped" being an understatement), and I was left standing there alone as row after row of automobiles drove by, with people from the performance putting their heads out the window and screaming, "Fuck yeah, Dave! Congratulations, mate! Excellent performance!" All I could do was smile and wave. What a moron.

I was shortly handcuffed, placed in the back of a police car, and brought across the street to a mobile police station, where I was interrogated by investigators as if I were Ted Bundy. "Can you tell me your home address?" What is the address of your mother's house? "Can you tell me where your mother works?" It went on for a long time, and if I did have a buzz, it was soon wearing off due to the monotonous and completely useless questioning. After what seemed like hours, I thought, "Just throw me in the goddamned cell." That is exactly what they did.

When I arrived at the jail, all of the other criminals from the show cheered me on as I was formally booked at the front desk and placed in a cell with a passed-out punter in a Primus T-shirt who snored so loudly that I thought I might have to hang myself with my shoelaces. Shivering from the chilly wet clothes I had been wearing all night in the rain, I retired to my concrete slab of a bed and did my best to put the stiff complementary canvas blanket they had given me around my body. Because the cell door was plexiglass, the room fell completely silent when it was closed, much like an acoustically treated vocal booth in a recording studio, so I just lay there listening to my ears ring from the triumphant show I had just performed, wondering how on earth my weekend in paradise had come to this.

Gus, my hero and rescuer, arrived a few hours later, and when he peered up at the security monitors full of prisoners, he pointed to my trembling figure on the screen and told the cops, "That one is mine." I'd been freed, and the ride back to our hotel was a cacophony of hilarity as I soberly recounted all of the immature events that had led to this very absurd fate. We slept for a few hours before flying to Sydney the next morning for a show that night.

But my criminal career was far from over. I was obligated by law to return to the Gold Coast a week later for my court date. If convicted, I would not only have to pay a fine, but I could also face jail time, not to mention jeopardise my chances of ever being able to visit their lovely nation again, which was the most terrible thought because Australia had become my favourite place to vacation over the years. I would never be able to forgive myself or my band if I blew that opportunity because of a few beers and a cheap scooter. I began to take this all very seriously, so seriously that Gus and I went to a department store and spent $700 on a suit so I wouldn't look like a complete jerk in front of the cops. Nothing is more pitiful than two adult men going through racks of clothes at a department store, making fashion selections based on the objectivity of a pompous judge, saying things like "Too conservative?" and "Too disco?" We settled on something dapper but not too rakish for our journey back north. The next day, as we were leaving the hotel in Melbourne to catch our flight back to Queensland, I ran into the guitarist of Primal Scream in the foyer, who said, "What do you call a Foo Fighter in a suit?" GUILTY!!!" This was ineffective.

We met my lawyer, or "barrister," as they are known in the legal world, at a Burger King near the courthouse and discussed my defence over greasy cheeseburgers and stale fries. There wasn't much else to say. I went over the speed limit in a car. The case is closed. There were no questionable technicalities on which I could rely to dismiss my case, so it was essentially up to the court to determine the harshness of my sentence (and the wisdom of my suit selection). We went over to the gallows for judgement day, and I straightened my cheap tie. This was becoming serious.

Before we even entered the building, I was confronted by a local TV crew, with a microphone probing my face as I walked and delivering "No comment" from behind my new sunglasses. If this whole ordeal has taught me anything, it's that I now understand what it's like to be Johnnie Cochran. Thank goodness that happened only once (and thank goodness I'm not Johnnie Cochran). At the very least, I thought, I look fine in this suit. We went inside and hoped for a "not guilty" decision, which seemed implausible.

The book was thrown at me by the judge. I luckily avoided jail time or community service, but technically it was a conviction, so I paid my fine (less than the suit!) and am now forever considered a criminal in Australia, which means that when I enter their country, I still have to check the little box that says, "HAVE YOU EVER BEEN CONVICTED OF A CRIME IN AUSTRALIA?" And every time I hand an immigration officer my form, they flip a small switch under their desk, illuminating a red light and summoning their supervisor to assist them. And every time I tell said supervisor about my crime, they laugh and say, "Oh, right! "I recall that!"

I THOUGHT I GOT OFF EASY. MY ACTUAL SENTENCE? LIFE IS RIDICULOUS.

If I had used my clairvoyant talent that night on the rainy highway, freezing in my hoodie as I approached the sobriety checkpoint, I wouldn't have had to answer for this shameful crime for years to come. Mine is a small cost to pay... But, ever since that meeting with the psychic in Sydney, I've wondered if the tremendous blue aura that appears to radiate from my calloused hands will ever aid me. Despite my alleged superpowers, I will always opt to let life run its natural course, a journey with no road map to refer to if you get lost.

CHAPTER 11
LIFE WAS PICKING UP SPEED

"How old are you?" the doctor inquired, perplexed.

"I'm forty," I said uncomfortably.

"And why are you here?" he asked.

"Because I'm having chest pains and I think I'm going to fucking die!" In a hurry, I shot back.

He flipped through the blurry digital images on the screen as we sat in front of the CT scan monitors at Cedars-Sinai hospital in Los Angeles, where I had just been subjected to lying perfectly still in a claustrophobic tube for half an hour, looking for any clogging or decay in the arteries and chambers of my strained heart. I sat beside him, wringing my sweating hands and waiting for my deadly diagnosis while he carefully scrutinised the seemingly indistinguishable black-and-white images for a minute or two, then sat back in his chair.

"Hmmmm . . . not really seeing anything here . . . are you under any stress?"

If only he knew, I thought. I almost fell out of my chair laughing at this slow-pitch question, but I answered him respectfully without making it appear so obvious.

"Ummm, yeah... a little bit," I responded, smirking.

"Do you get much sleep?"

"Maybe three to four hours a night?" I replied sheepishly, which was, to be fair, a rather generous assessment at the moment.

"Do you drink a lot of coffee?" he inquired after another swing.

Bingo!

"Define a lot of coffee...," I responded, knowing that my caffeine consumption would definitely cause Juan Valdez to pack his donkey and flee to the Colombian hills. I was almost ashamed to mention how much coffee I drank in a day for fear of him 5150ing me and sending me off in a straitjacket to the nearest Caffeine Anonymous meeting. I'd only lately recognized my addiction, admitting that maybe five pots of coffee a day was a little excessive, but I hadn't embraced the catastrophic repercussions until now. Regrettably, I am THAT man. Give me one, and I'll take 10. There's a reason I've never done cocaine, because I know deep down that if I used coke the way I drink coffee, I'd be sucking dicks at the bus stop every morning for an eight ball. Coffee. Just typing the term makes me hungry. Let's just say I'm no connoisseur, I just need the fix. Hot, cold, gourmet, gas station, fresh brewed, bottom of the pot, instant, French press... I'm the furthest thing from a coffee snob (a pretentious sect that I despise), so I'll drink whatever is available. I've had it all, from Dunkin' Donuts to the world's most costly bean, harvested from the faeces of wild civets in Southeast Asia, and I drink it for one purpose and one reason only: to get high.

But it wasn't only the coffee that sent me to the hospital on that particular day. Life was accelerating. 2009 was a fantastic year. It all started with my 40th birthday party, which was held at the Medieval Times theme restaurant in Anaheim, California, a massive equestrian arena where you can watch fake knights with fake English accents joust while eating greasy turkey legs with your bare hands and drinking Coors Light from BeDazzled chalices. It is the most absurd, hilarious, and downright embarrassing dining experience known to man, and apparently not somewhere a grown man would typically celebrate another trip around the sun, which I didn't realise until the fake king's voice came booming over the PA with a few announcements. "Ladies and gentlemen, tonight we have a few birthdays!" Eddie is seven years old! Tommy is ten years old! And Dave is about to turn... forty?"

I got down behind my set and made minor tweaks as John warmed up his fingers on the bass, ripping the most bizarre phrases with ease, and then I joined in with his groove, locking in so precisely, so fluidly, that I thought to myself, WOW! Right now, I'm fucking murdering it!! But I soon discovered that it wasn't me who was making the drums sound good; it was John. His ability to lock onto the drums and stick to every beat was incredible, making the groove flow so much smoother and stronger than anything else I had ever encountered with a bassist. That's when I realised this experiment was going to work. It was only a matter of seconds after Josh joined in that we recognized this was meant to be. Now there was no turning back. We jammed for a few days, getting to know each other while ordering out from Kids Castle (or, as we jokingly called it, Kids Asshole), feeling each other out and writing a few riffs, eventually coming up with a master plan to pursue this new musical union: we would meet in L.A. for two weeks to write and record, disperse and retreat to our corners for a small break, and then reconvene and continue to build an arsenal. It had become official. LIFE WAS SPEEDING UP.

In the meantime, my day job called. After a year and a half on the road, the Foo Fighters were asked to create and record a new song to include in the tracklist to help promote the greatest hits collection (otherwise known as "the song on the greatest hits record that is neither great nor a hit"). Discussions began about how, when, and with whom we would record it, and because I was officially in two bands, this scheduling required some logistical wrangling. I wasn't sure when or how we'd do it, but I knew who I wanted to do it with: my old pal Butch Vig. Butch and I had a storied history and had always been close, but we hadn't worked together since Nirvana's Nevermind in 1991. For years, I was hesitant to collaborate with Butch again, fearing that the lengthy shadow cast by Nirvana after Kurt's death would invalidate any of my own music. Whatever we filmed together would only be compared to what we had done previously, which has been a burden I have had to shoulder since the day we met. As much as I adored Butch, and despite the fact that he is one of the best producers of all time and the drummer of alt-rock legends Garbage, I didn't want that weight to overshadow what should have been a joyful reunion. Butch's method is straightforward: obtain huge sounds, play big riffs, and build a big song. That's all. It was often difficult to determine if he was even working because the guy is so laid-back and relaxed that you forget you're working. It was easy to forget, with his thick Wisconsin accent and kind studio manner, that he had produced some of the biggest rock albums of all time for Nirvana, Smashing Pumpkins, and Green Day, to mention a few. But, after some considerable soul searching, I resolved to disregard what the naysayers would say and give it my all. As with most things in my life, I revel in the absurdity of it all and seize every bizarre moment, so what better place to gather 150 of my closest friends, all seated in the arena's "Blue Knight" section, drunkenly cheering on our noble chevalier with bloodthirsty abandon, praying for a kill? And what better time to form a band than the night I brought Led Zeppelin's bassist, John Paul Jones, to my old friend Josh Homme to kick off our new, top-secret project, Them Crooked Vultures?

I met Josh in the early 1990s while he was playing guitar in one of my favourite bands of all time, Kyuss, and we had since toured the world together with his band Queens of the Stone Age, which I had even joined for a short time, recording their album Songs for the Deaf and playing some of the most explosive shows of my entire life. Josh has "the thing," an indefinable, unspoken, magical ability that is truly one in a million, and whenever we played together, the result was always like a hypnotic wave of starlings, the music effortlessly flowing from one direction to the next, never losing its tight pattern. Our onstage improvisation was like two old friends finishing each other's sentences, frequently laughing uncontrollably behind each other's back at our musical inside jokes. In essence, it was a match made in heaven, and we would seize any opportunity to join forces. We discussed a side project from time to time, generally when we were fatigued from our day jobs' commitments and obligations, and when our bands crossed paths on tour. Over cartons of cigarettes and gallons of backstage cocktails, we'd sit about fantasising about something strange, loose, and entertaining. Josh was also a drummer, so we could simply switch instruments while attempting to move as far away from the sound of Queens and the Foos as possible. But we knew we'd have a good time, and after a year and a half on the road playing "Learn to Fly" every single night, the promise of something exciting was much needed to keep me from abandoning music and being the terrible roofer I was destined to be. Around the same time, I was asked to present the members of Led Zeppelin with a GQ Outstanding Achievement Award (let the painfully obvious sentiment of that colossal understatement sink in for a moment), so I called Josh and asked if I should mention the idea of our secret project to John Paul Jones, the greatest, grooviest bassist in rock and roll history. "You know John Paul Jones?" he inquired. I had previously recorded with him for the Foo Fighters' album In Your Honor in 2004. He also conducted the orchestra during a performance at the Foos Grammys. He was not only friendly and down-to-earth, but also a musical genius. He'd also worked as a producer for musicians such as the amazing Butthole Surfers and Diamanda Galás. The guy wasn't afraid to become crazy, to say the least, so there was a chance he'd agree to our bizarre plan. If the magic that Josh and I had together was combined with the all-powerful John Paul Jones, we'd have a "supergroup" (a silly name that we avoided). What the hell, Josh and I reasoned, it was worth a shot, and before long, I was standing face-to-face with John at the prize ceremony, timidly whispering the suggestion into his ear. He didn't say yes, but he also didn't say no, so we decided to keep in touch via email and see if we could come up with something. I flew home giddy with excitement at the possibility of really playing drums with a man who had once played alongside the drummer who had most influenced me. I could only hope he'd take our offer, but I wasn't holding my breath because, well, he was John Paul Jones.

Lo and behold, John decided to make the trip out to Los Angeles to see if we had the chemistry that I had imagined we would have, and his arrival coincided with my fantastically juvenile birthday party, so I invited him along for a mediaeval feast of greasy fast-food delights. Poor man, he was about to be thrown into a disgusting, Americanized version of the Middle Ages while his host and future bandmate got cross-eyed drunk, smoking joints in the men's room between staged jousting bouts. If he can make it through this night of lowbrow theatre and youthful antics without crashing at LAX, we might have a chance at something amazing. Bless his heart, he patiently tolerated my immaturity, and we met a few days later at Josh's studio, Pink Duck, for our first jam. Give Butch a call. Life is too brief to allow someone else's viewpoint to guide the wheel, I reasoned. The calendars were released, and no matter how hard we tried to find spare time, the Foos sessions had to overlap with previously booked Them Crooked Vultures sessions. We felt I could pull it off if I recorded with the Foos from eleven a.m. to six p.m. and then raced to the Vultures' studio from seven p.m. to midnight. No problem, I reasoned. When I die, I'll sleep! After all, nothing a few additional cups of coffee a day couldn't fix! So, in order to achieve this insane goal, I quickly increased my consumption of that dirty, black daily grind to dangerous levels. Oh, and I had a second child. Harper Willow Grohl arrived in the world on April 17, 2009. From the start, she was a screaming ball of joy, so wonderful, so gorgeous. My understanding of love grew tenfold with her arrival, and I was once again a proud parent. I'd always loved life, but my new daughter made me love it even more, waking up enthusiastically every morning to see her gorgeous face, no matter how sleep deprived I was. As any parent will confirm, the miracle of a newborn takes precedence over all other aspects of your life, and you forget about your own survival because you are fully focused on theirs, an ethos that my mother surely displayed during my childhood years. I was happy to now have two beautiful girls and would jump at any chance to spend time with them, day or night, no matter how weary I was from my insane schedule of rushing from one studio to the next all day, drinking coffee like it was an Olympic event. LIFE WAS SPEEDING UP.

As if all of this wasn't enough to send me to my death (HERE LIES DAVID ERIC GROHL. HE SHOULD HAVE SWITCHED TO SANKA), the Foo Fighters were invited to perform at the White House for a July 4 barbecue hosted by freshly elected President Obama for our military families. It was an opportunity I couldn't pass up, set on the groomed South Lawn overlooking the monuments of the National Mall, for a variety of personal reasons. After all, this was my hometown, and I'd spent countless Fourth of Julys on the other side of that White House fence, watching the magnificent fireworks display above from a blanket in the grass while the Beach Boys played on a festival stage in the distance, or attending punk rock concerts at the base of the Lincoln Memorial as an angry teenager, exercising my right to protest on the day when it might have meant the most. But this was unique. This was a personal invitation to join our first African American president in his backyard to honour the men and women who defend our right to rejoice, protest, and elect our leaders through democratic means. This was more than simply a cookout; it was an honour. In addition, I was refurbishing my home. With my ever-expanding family, my once-large house began to seem cramped. So plans were established to transform previously insignificant rooms into something more kid-friendly (and... ahem... a studio for myself where we would one day record our album Wasting Light). Violet was three years old at the time, and Harper was just three months old, so considerable rearrangement was required to accommodate them, which necessitated some major work. Construction is quite loud. There is only one way to describe it: fucking chaos. With a driveway that looked like valet parking at a Dodge vehicle convention and scores of workers brandishing power tools that elevated the decibel level to Motörhead-worthy levels, there is only one way to describe it: fucking insanity. LIFE WAS SPEEDING UP.

My new schedule went something like this for weeks: A baby and a three-year-old demanding my complete attention at the crack of dawn, while buzz saws and jackhammers thunder in the distance. Make yourself a cup of coffee. Drink the coffee and dash straight to the Foo Fighters' studio. Make yourself another cup of coffee. Begin working. Drink that cup of coffee, but also a cup of strong made iced tea in between, believing that this is hydration. Make another pot of coffee so I can drink some on my way to the next studio (road soda). Arrive in the Vultures' studio, throw on another pot, and consume that for the next four hours while I bash the living shit out of my drums in an attempt to impress John Paul Jones. Drive home, trembling like a leaf from the four thousand milligrams of caffeine I've just taken over the course of eighteen hours, and try unsuccessfully to get at least four hours of sleep before waking up and repeating the process. And so forth, ad nauseam, on loop. LIFE WAS SPEEDING UP.

This unpleasant moment of my developing dilemma is best appreciated by seeing the now-infamous YouTube clip "Fresh Pots," a two-minute short film put together by our old friend and comrade Liam Lynch, who was present during the Vultures record's production. He was there to document the creative process of our secret project when he witnessed my collapse and gathered my most crazy moments into a hilarious (and embarrassing) video that he intended to reveal exclusively to the band. When the first Vultures single was finally published, the band didn't have a music video to promote it, so my manager asked if we could instead release the "Fresh Pots" clip. Although it was embarrassing, I decided to take one for the team and let the world witness a man in the throes of a full-on caffeine binge acting like a total madman. Nobody will ever see it, I reasoned. I was mistaken. I was in the grocery store the day after it came out, and the kid bagging my goods glanced up at me and said, "Hey, man... want a cup of coffee?" Fuck. It has nearly seven million views as of this writing. I recall the first ache. I was in my hallway at home, fretting about the deafening remodelling that shook the house like dropping bombs, when it hit me like a knife in my rib cage. I came to a halt and lifted my palm to my chest, scared that I was suffering a heart attack but hoping it was simply a torn muscle from all of the drumming I'd been doing with the Vultures. But something told me it wasn't a strained muscle. I'd already pulled them all. This was coming from a deeper place. I took a few deep breaths to see if it would go away, but it didn't. It persisted. Without sounding the alarm and running around the house yelling, "THIS IS THE BIG ONE!!" like Fred Sanford, I calmly opened my laptop and mistakenly searched "symptoms of a heart attack." (I now know better than to self-diagnose using a random blogger's homemade website.) I didn't have ALL of the symptoms, but I was clearly feeling something serious, so I looked up heart attack prevention methods and chose to keep it a secret. After all, I wasn't going to miss this White House gig for anything. Even a heart attack couldn't keep me from flying home and performing for the president. I slipped two aspirin in my wallet and didn't say anything. LIFE WAS SPEEDING UP.

When I arrived at the White House, the lovely heat of DC's oppressive summer air almost healed the anguish in my chest, and as we prepared to soundcheck on the lawn, I looked out over the fence to the monuments I had once taken for granted. The Washington Monument, looming in the distance like a maypole around which the city performs its intricate dance. In the annual rebirth of spring, the Jefferson Memorial is graced by rows of cherry blossoms. And the Lincoln Memorial, where I went to numerous Fourth of July performances as a teenage punk rocker. These were not the Beach Boys; they were protest songs. The "Rock Against Reagan" concert, performed every Fourth of July during his presidency, was a gathering of punks from all over who came to sing along with their favourite bands in unison in opposition to the president's ultraconservative policies. I was no political science major, but I did participate in and offer my voice to the fight for the freedom to express myself anyway I saw fit. After Reagan departed office, the event was renamed "Rock Against Racism," and I went to each of those shows with the same zeal and purpose. This memory stuck with me that day because not only was I on the opposite side of the fence on the Fourth of July, but so was President Obama. LIFE WAS SPEEDING UP.

Our road crew dressed formally, wearing black cargo shorts instead of black sweatpants, and as the stage was being set up, we all became friends with the kind White House security guards and electricians. "If you guys need to use the restrooms, there's one over there and one over there," said one wise man. Don't pee in the bushes under any circumstances. People are hiding in the bushes." Noted.

We were escorted up to the house for the first time to meet Barack Obama, and as we walked into the Blue Room, overlooking the grill below, we were welcomed by the president and First Lady with a really down-to-earth, friendly, and kind greeting. We chatted and laughed casually, almost forgetting that we were standing with the president and First Lady, Michelle (who, to be honest, seemed more presidential than the president himself). Pat wasn't his usual, easygoing self as we stood there talking and snapping pictures. He appeared quiet, which was unusual for him. When we arrived back at the South Lawn, he explained why. Pat was visiting the White House for the first time, a place where his great-grandfather, a former slave, once waited in line to greet and shake hands with Abraham Lincoln. Our visit to the White House had taken on new significance. That night, as we watched the fireworks from the balcony, I was overcome with emotion when I gazed up at the First Family standing on the balcony. History was being written. And as I saw my wife, children, and mother's lighted faces staring up into the sky, I was thrilled with pride, pleased to share this historic moment with them. And I was flooded with affection for Pat, my most trusted and loyal buddy. We'd all gotten over the fence together. LIFE WAS SPEEDING UP.

When I got back to Los Angeles, I called my doctor right away. "Dude, I've been having some chest pains," I explained. "Are you having them right now??" he asked, sounding more concerned than usual (and that's a lot). "Ummm... kinda...," I responded. He urged me to get in the car and drive to his office right away, so I sped out the door like Moses. I stormed into his office and was soon lying on a table, being poked and prodded and connected up like a vintage synthesiser. "Hmmmm... not seeing anything here... let's get you on the treadmill and then we'll do an ultrasound..." he stated as the paper printout from the EKG spilled onto the floor. I was transported to another floor, where I was again coated in small electro-patches and urged to jog like the Six Million Dollar Man on a treadmill. Then I leaped onto a table, where they slathered me in gel and used an ultrasound wand to watch my heart throb. "Hmmmm . . . not seeing anything here . . . let's get you over to Cedars for a CT scan . . ." I was beginning to feel like the little girl from The Exorcist, forced to test after test when it was actually just a simple demonic possession. Perhaps I needed a priest? After meeting with the doctor at Cedars and determining that there was no genuine threat, he advised me to take it easy. Even though I felt invincible, I was no superman, and I needed to take care of myself in order to take care of those I cared about. My love of life could be a little too much at times, pushing myself a little too far, but if I wanted to stay around for a while, I needed to be more aware of my mortal boundaries. What is his prescription? "Play drums only three times a week, have a glass of wine before bed, and lay off the coffee."

TWO OUT OF THREE IS NOT A BAD RATIO. DECAF IS AMAZING. And life is still accelerating.

CHAPTER 12
SWING DANCING WITH AC/DC

"Do you mind if AC/DC comes to dinner?"

This text from my wife, Jordyn, will go down in history as the most bizarre, absurd, and painfully apparent question I have ever been asked. AC/DC during dinner? The band that almost never appears in public, only to materialise on gigantic stages equipped with massive exploding cannons and massive amplifiers packed to the rafters? For almost forty years, the band has symbolised fist-pumping, headbanging, foot-stomping bad-boy boogie with an outlaw's grin and a devilish wink. Not to mention selling over 200 million albums and motivating generations of teenage rockers to dedicate their lives to three chords and a tattered pair of jeans? I should be aware. I was among them. Let There Be Rock was released in 1980 in an unknowing world of overly glamorised pop music, and it immediately made its way to all of the hip movie houses across the country that screened midnight movies on weekends. (A long-forgotten phenomena that most of my generation remembers as a stoner rite of passage. Some of my favourites were The Rocky Horror Picture Show, The Wall, and Heavy Metal.) The film is a tour de force, with the world's grittiest, grooviest no-bullshit hard rock band offering up a megadose of sweat, denim, and high-voltage rock and roll. It was filmed in Paris only a few months before the death of their original lead vocalist, Bon Scott. If you wanted to learn how to kick fucking ass and take fucking names, this was the master class for you. I was already familiar with AC/DC at eleven years old, since their albums Dirty Deeds Done Dirt Cheap and Highway to Hell were two of my most treasured CDs in my increasing collection, so this movie was something I had to see. The Washington Post reported that the video was screened as part of the Wall of Sound concert series at the historic Uptown Theater in Washington, DC. So Larry Hinkle, my best buddy at the time, and I made a night of it, chauffeured downtown by his father in their burgundy Datsun 280ZX, the poor man's Porsche. I was expecting a theatre full of denim-and-leather-clad hoodlums as Larry and I were dropped off at the ticket booth. When we entered, however, I discovered that there were only a few hard-core AC/DC fans there, scattered in small groups throughout the rows and rows of empty seats, waiting for the film to start while unsuccessfully attempting to conceal the flickering lighters that were sparking their pinner joints and homemade pipes. We attempted to determine where to sit, like two shy kids in a socially oppressive lunchroom, because the place was nearly empty and we were worried of getting a contact high from the sweet-smelling pot wafting throughout the auditorium. Knowing it was the Wall of Sound concert series, we were tempted to sit near the sound system up front, but we chose a seat further back so we wouldn't have to strain our slender necks to see the enormous screen. Thank goodness, since we had no idea there was a concert-sized PA hiding behind those curtains, and as the house lights went down, it became clear that this was no ordinary matinée showing of Star Wars.

The film begins with a rogue road crew of beefy, long-haired hooligans demolishing a rock and roll stage before putting it into a fleet of trucks and transporting it to the next city for another night of mayhem. This was something I'd never seen or thought about before. After the last note of a concert has been played and the audience has gone home to the comfort of their warm beds, it's these brave souls who go to work coiling miles of cables and packing tons of equipment into battered road cases while wading through your littered beer cups and cigarette butts before passing out in bunks the size of coffins, getting just enough sleep to set it all back up the next morning. This nicely set the tone for what Larry and I were about to witness. This was not the glamour we'd been conditioned to associate with the larger-than-life rock stars on our bedroom walls; this was the real thing, and all those years of imagining rock and roll to be life's most colourful theatre faded into ripped T-shirts and bloody knuckles. As the trucks barreled down the highway, blasting their air horns, it was clear that the theatre's PA system was on "stun." I mean, this was DEAFENING. And we hadn't even started on the music. It was without a doubt the loudest thing I had ever heard in my eleven years on Earth. I had never gone to a rock concert before, so I had no idea the strength of that level of noise could shake your rib cage with earthquake intensity. Needless to say, it appealed to me. A lot. My ears were already ringing by the time the band took the stage with their first song, "Live Wire," and I was on the edge of my seat.

I WANTED TO RIP THAT THEATRE TO SHREDS.

The adrenaline coursing through my veins triggered what can only be described as the change that Bruce Banner would go through when transforming into the Hulk in the late 1970s TV series. I couldn't stop myself from feeling overwhelmed and empowered by the sheer intensity of the music. I would have ripped the seat out of the floor and smashed it in the aisle if my skinny little arms had the strength, but instead I sat there shivering in my sneakers as AC/DC did what they do best: give every ounce of themselves to the audience and leave nothing behind.

Within a few songs, the drummer is seen replacing his snare drum after breaking it from too much rocking. Whoa. Angus Young, soaked in perspiration, can be seen on the side of the stage with an oxygen mask in between songs since he just ran at least three marathons from one side of the stage to the other over the course of thirteen songs and his body could barely withstand the rock. Oh my god. This was incredible, I thought. Forget about the bands who merely stood there and fiddled with their instruments like mediaeval minstrels; these guys assaulted them as if it were their final day on Earth. I was a different boy by the time the credits rolled. I THOUGHT IF I'M GOING TO PLAY MUSIC IN A BAND, I'M GOING TO DO IT LIKE THAT.

I responded to Jordyn's text with a huge "DUH" and pinch myself for finally getting to meet the band who inspired me to kick fucking ass and take fucking names. If you've ever been to a Scream, Nirvana, or Foo Fighters concert, you'll understand where this intensity comes from. Let There Be Rock by AC/DC is responsible for everything.

AC/DC happened to be in town in 2015 to perform their new song "Rock or Bust" at the 57th Annual Grammy Awards. I wasn't performing that night; instead, I was presenting an award, but as a lifelong AC/DC fan, I was far more anxious to see them than any of the other pretty monotonous pop acts with their absurd, Vegas-style displays. The show needed a big dose of good old-fashioned rock and roll. I'd be there, front and centre, feeling the same overwhelming rush of adrenaline that had made me want to rip the Uptown Theater to shreds 35 years before (except now I'd be shoulder to shoulder with Katy Perry and Tony Bennett, feeling like I was hiding my flickering lighter at the end of a homemade pipe).

I contacted Taylor and Pat to invite them to a post-show dinner with our spouses, choosing out of the traditional after-parties, which are generally just orgies of selfies and industry small talk, because I was going to be there on my own without my beloved Foo Fighters. We reserved a table at Faith and Flower, a restaurant just a few blocks from the theatre, and planned to meet for dinner and drinks away from the crowds after the event. Paul McCartney was also in town and inquired about our plans for the evening, so we kindly invited him and his wife Nancy, adding two more chairs to our growing table. Any night with Paul is a fantastic night in my opinion, so this was shaping up to be an awesome evening. Apparently, Paul ran into the AC/DC guys at the hotel, and when asked what was up next, he indicated he was having dinner with us, which led to my life's most bizarre SMS.

Pause. Reflect.

I NEVER GO A DAY WITHOUT THANKING THE UNIVERSE FOR THESE OTHERWORLDLY BLESSINGS, AND I MAKE IT A POINT TO TAKE NOTHING FOR GRANTED. Being a part of such a waking dream will never feel "normal" to me; it will always feel like I'm witnessing life from above, looking down at someone else's fantasy unfolding before me. But it is mine, and it is at these moments that I strive to be present, reminding myself that I am possibly the luckiest person on the planet to be able to take the next breath that will bring me to the next adventure.

I received another text a few days before the show from my dear buddy Ben Jaffe of New Orleans' famed Preservation Hall Jazz Band, informing me that he was also in town for the Grammys and looking for a party. Nobody parties like a true New Orleans native, and nothing says New Orleans more than the Preservation Hall Jazz Band. Ben's father, Allan, founded them in the early 1960s, and they have epitomised the music, energy, and joy of their great city, keeping traditional New Orleans jazz alive for almost sixty years, playing three performances a night, three hundred sixty-five days a year. So, even when they put down their instruments (which they rarely do), the party never stops. In 2014, Foo Fighters had the distinction of spending a week recording their documentary series Sonic Highways in Preservation Hall, a pub that dates back to 1803. We all quickly became fast friends. By the end of that week, I had come to the conclusion that New Orleans is an American gem, and that we must all work together to preserve its unique culture steeped in European, Caribbean, and Cajun past. There is no place on Earth that has the absolute magic that New Orleans does. Without a question, it is my favourite city in the world.

"Dude . . . we're having dinner with Paul McCartney AND AC/DC!" Ben, I exclaimed. "You wanna come along?" I knew Ben would understand the magnitude of such an awesome unexpected encounter. "Can I bring all of the guys with me?" he inquired. I took a breather and performed the maths. The Preservation Hall Jazz Band had seven players, which indicated that at least 10 more people were needed. Of course, I would have loved to have them all, but we were on our way to taking over the entire fucking restaurant, so I responded with a timid "Uh, let me check," fearful that the restaurant would refuse our request for another 10 chairs. But then he sealed the deal by saying: "How about we all come marching down the street playing in a second line, into the restaurant, straight to the table, and perform a set for you right there?"

There was no way to turn down such a great offer. A second-line parade is a distinctive New Orleans art form, a practice dating back to the nineteenth century in which a brass band marches down the street behind a funeral procession to celebrate the life of a lost loved one. Today, more informal versions of these parades may be found at any time on the streets of New Orleans, and if you hear the sound of syncopated funked-up jazz-swing approaching, grab a drink and join in. You never know where it will take you. I assured Ben that I would make this happen come hell or high water, and that we should keep it a secret so that we could surprise all of our honoured guests with a night they would never forget (not to mention the entire restaurant, whispering over plates of high cuisine, who would surely be taken aback by the sheer volume of New Orleans' most beloved band's howling horns, crashing cymbals, and thundering tubas).

Our calm little table had now been relocated to a private room in the back, large enough to comfortably accommodate our ever-expanding guest list in a space large enough for us all to grab a partner and swing them around the floor in a night of drunken celebration. I couldn't wait to see everyone's expressions as the band marched into the room, hoping for the similar feeling I'd had the first time I joined in on a second line in New Orleans. A sense of belonging and love, shared with people from all walks of life, united in rhythm and delight as we followed the music wherever it took us. On my first day in New Orleans, I was dancing down the street with strangers, smiling and bouncing to the music, when I noticed a familiar face, Ben Jaffe, standing on top of a car in the distance. We'd only met a few days before, yet he hopped down, gave me the warmest hug, turned to a man selling beer and minibar bottles of wine from a wheeled cooler, and purchased us beverages for our afternoon drive. At eleven a.m., Sutter Home rosé had never tasted so nice. He suddenly became my lifelong brother. Jordyn and I dashed over to the restaurant after the Grammys to beat the crowd before our spectacular evening began. Our secret was mainly safe, but Paul was aware of it because, well, he is the all-knowing, all-seeing, omniscient, and almighty Paul McCartney. It turns out Paul had a relationship with Preservation Hall dating back to his time in Wings, when he recorded at local icon Allen Toussaint's studio and would stop over to hang. "He was a sort of regular for a while," Ben explained. I kept my phone nearby to coordinate the time of the band's entrance, ensuring sure everything was ready for the big reveal. The room began to fill up with the familiar faces of the individuals I care about the most. My mother, my pals, Paul... and then they appeared... AC/DC in person. To be honest, I had previously met singer Brian Johnson, albeit briefly, at a hotel bar in Valencia, Spain, on a day off from our Foo Fighters tour in 1996. We flowed out of the bus after a long drive on a day off and observed a few denim-clad autograph seekers standing out front with stacks of photos and magazines to be signed. Standard procedure for any travelling band, but when we approached, we realised that they were completely engulfed in AC/DC paraphernalia and had no idea who we were. "You guys must love AC/DC!" I chuckled as we passed, and they revealed in their thick Spanish accents that AC/DC was staying in our hotel since they were performing at the nearby Plaza de Toros de las Ventas bullfighting stadium that night, which happened to be a rare night off for us. I dashed to my room and called our tour manager, insisting that we all receive tickets for this gig, which would be my first time seeing an AC/DC concert. We made a few phone calls and were able to secure enough passes for everyone. We went from room to room, making plans to meet in the hotel bar for some pre-show cocktails before heading down to the event.

As we sipped our drinks at the hotel bar, a man in black pants, a black T-shirt, and a flat cap stepped into the beautiful room and ordered himself a drink while sitting alone on a barstool. We went motionless, stunned, since there was none other than THE Brian Johnson, the man who performed "Have a Drink on Me" from AC/DC's most popular album, Back in Black. Brian turned to us as the bartender handed him his glass, and with a wink and a smile, he raised his glass in a simple toast, just saying, "Lads!" We all lifted our glasses to him, appreciating the poetry of this magnificent occasion. I'm quite sure he mistook us for his road crew, but I was on cloud nine. That night, I finally got to see the AC/DC I fell in love with as an eleven-year-old dorky rock-and-roll worshipper. The amount of enthusiasm they demonstrated onstage was precisely what I had imagined, with Angus Young sprinting from one end of the massive stage decked with pyrotechnics and exploding cannons. The packed house only added to the spectacle, singing not just every line but also the guitar sections as they bounced like a rolling human wave to the rhythm of each song. It was awe-inspiring. Seeing all of these extremely prominent faces stream into our ramshackle after-Grammys party would have been enough to make me die happy, but knowing what was to come made it even sweeter. There was no way I could repay this room full of icons for the years of inspiration they had provided me, but if I could make them smile, dance, and feel the joy of music, like they had done for me my entire life, I would have made a little dent in my debt. As the celebration in our back room grew louder, I checked my phone and saw a text from Ben: "We're down the block in our van, dressed and ready to go!" It was finally time. "Bring it," I said, shakily taking my spot at the window that looked out onto the street, waiting to see the band in their trademark black suits and ties dance down the sidewalk toward the restaurant. I heard the faint sound of that classic New Orleans swing in the distance a few moments later, and as they rounded the corner, the hair on my arms sprang up at the sight of them shuffling toward the front door in time. Within seconds, the restaurant was filled with the deafening sound of brass as it made its way past the tables of stunned customers. Conversation in our small group came to a halt as everyone tried to figure out what the hell was going on in the other room, and suddenly... The Preservation Hall Jazz Band came into the room and took its place in the centre of the floor, surrounded by the bemused faces of our guests, as they blew their trumpets with frenzied zeal, barely feet from our shaking eardrums. After the first shock wore off, the little floor transformed into a ballroom, and everyone dropped their drinks to take their partners for a spin around the room. All of the rock and roll pretence and nobility vanished in that moment, and all that remained was pure delight. As we danced, Brian Johnson turned to face me and said, "I'M ACTUALLY FUCKING HAPPY!!"

My task here was completed. More music, more cocktails, and more joy filled the night. It was also a sort of reunion, with Paul and Ben reminiscing about Paul's time in New Orleans years ago and his friendship with Ben's late father, which must have meant a lot to Ben. At one point, Paul took up a trumpet and began to play "When the Saints Go Marching In," and the band naturally joined in and played along. "My first instrument was the trumpet!" Paul stated to Ben. Then my mother bought me a guitar, and you know how the rest of the tale goes..."

Yes, we most emphatically do. The night continued until the early hours, and no matter how much we thought it would never end, the house lights came on, and it was time to return to reality, which seemed so far away after such a magnificent evening. I WAS EXHAUSTED—NOT PHYSICALLY, BUT MY SOUL HAD JUST FINISHED A TRIATHLON OF EMOTION, NOSTALGIA, AND ENDLESS LOVE FOR MUSIC. It's difficult to put into words my faith in music. It is good for me. A supernatural mystery in whose strength I will always have complete faith. And it is times like this that strengthen my faith. Don't only listen when you hear the procession coming down the street, spreading pleasure and love with every note; engage in the march. You never know where it will take you.

To be honest, I had previously met singer Brian Johnson, albeit briefly, at a hotel bar in Valencia, Spain, on a day off from our Foo Fighters tour in 1996. We flowed out of the bus after a long drive on a day off and observed a few denim-clad autograph seekers standing out front with stacks of photos and magazines to be signed. Standard procedure for any travelling band, but when we approached, we realised that they were completely engulfed in AC/DC paraphernalia and had no idea who we were. "You guys must love AC/DC!" I chuckled as we passed, and they revealed in their thick Spanish accents that AC/DC was staying in our hotel since they were performing at the nearby Plaza de Toros de las Ventas bullfighting stadium that night, which happened to be a rare night off for us. I dashed to my room and called our tour manager, insisting that we all receive tickets for this gig, which would be my first time seeing an AC/DC concert. We made a few phone calls and were able to secure enough passes for everyone. We went from room to room, making plans to meet in the hotel bar for some pre-show cocktails before heading down to the event.

As we sipped our drinks at the hotel bar, a man in black pants, a black T-shirt, and a flat cap stepped into the beautiful room and ordered himself a drink while sitting alone on a barstool. We went motionless, stunned, since there was none other than THE Brian Johnson, the man who performed "Have a Drink on Me" from AC/DC's most popular album, Back in Black. Brian turned to us as the bartender handed him his glass, and with a wink and a smile, he raised his glass in a simple toast, just saying, "Lads!" We all lifted our glasses to him, appreciating the poetry of this magnificent occasion. I'm quite sure he mistook us for his road crew, but I was on cloud nine. That night, I finally got to see the AC/DC I fell in love with as an eleven-year-old dorky rock-and-roll worshipper. The amount of enthusiasm they demonstrated onstage was precisely what I had imagined, with Angus Young sprinting from one end of the massive stage decked with pyrotechnics and exploding cannons. The packed house only added to the spectacle, singing not just every line but also the guitar sections as they bounced like a rolling human wave to the rhythm of each song. It was awe-inspiring.

Seeing all of these extremely prominent faces stream into our ramshackle after-Grammys party would have been enough to make me die happy, but knowing what was to come made it even sweeter. There was no way I could repay this room full of icons for the years of inspiration they had provided me, but if I could make them smile, dance, and feel the joy of music, like they had done for me my entire life, I would have made a little dent in my debt.

As the celebration in our back room grew louder, I checked my phone and saw a text from Ben: "We're down the block in our van, dressed and ready to go!" It was finally time. "Bring it," I said, shakily taking my spot at the window that looked out onto the street, waiting to see the band in their trademark black suits and ties dance down the sidewalk toward the restaurant. I heard the faint sound of that classic New Orleans swing in the distance a few moments later, and as they rounded the corner, the hair on my arms sprang up at the sight of them shuffling toward the front door in time. Within seconds, the restaurant was filled with the deafening sound of brass as it made its way past the tables of stunned customers. Conversation in our small group came to a halt as everyone tried to figure out what the hell was going on in the other room, and suddenly... The Preservation Hall Jazz Band came into the room and took its place in the centre of the floor, surrounded by the bemused faces of our guests, as they blew their trumpets with frenzied zeal, barely feet from our shaking eardrums. After the first shock wore off, the little floor transformed into a ballroom, and everyone dropped their drinks to take their partners for a spin around the room. All of the rock and roll pretence and nobility vanished in that moment, and all that remained was pure delight. As we danced, Brian Johnson turned to face me and said, "I'M ACTUALLY FUCKING HAPPY!!"

My task here was completed.

More music, more cocktails, and more joy filled the night. It was also a sort of reunion, with Paul and Ben reminiscing about Paul's time in New Orleans years ago and his friendship with Ben's late father, which must have meant a lot to Ben. At one point, Paul took up a trumpet and began to play "When the Saints Go Marching In," and the band naturally joined in and played along. "My first instrument was the trumpet!" Paul stated to Ben. Then my mother bought me a guitar, and you know how the rest of the tale goes..."

Yes, we most emphatically do.

The night continued until the early hours, and no matter how much we thought it would never end, the house lights came on, and it was time to return to reality, which seemed so far away after such a magnificent evening. I WAS EXHAUSTED—NOT PHYSICALLY, BUT MY SOUL HAD JUST FINISHED A TRIATHLON OF EMOTION, NOSTALGIA, AND ENDLESS LOVE FOR MUSIC. It's difficult to put into words my faith in music. It is good for me. A supernatural mystery in whose strength I will always have complete faith. And it is times like this that strengthen my faith.

Don't only listen when you hear the procession coming down the street, spreading pleasure and love with every note; engage in the march. You never know where it will take you.

CHAPTER 13
INSPIRED, YET AGAIN

"Excuse me, are you Dave Grohl?"

I took a deep drag off my cigarette and nodded as I stood at the curb outside the LAX departure terminal, waiting to board my aircraft to Seattle. "Yep." "I read in an interview that the only person you ever really wanted to meet was Little Richard," the young man smiled. Is that correct?"

"Absolutely," I said. "He's the originator."

"Well, he's my dad," he explained.

I backed up, threw my cigarette to the ground, and shook the man's hand with a crushing hold, honoured and amazed to meet the son of rock and roll's great pioneer.

"Do you want to meet him?" He's in the car right now... "

I couldn't even speak. This was the moment I had been looking forward to. Little Richard has always been the most significant person I've ever met or will ever meet on God's green world. Without Little Richard, there would be no rock & roll. & there would be no me without rock & roll. The young man tapped the tinted glass of the limousine parked on the curb beside us as we took a few steps. He leaned in, whispering quietly to the person behind the glass as it lowered a few inches. The window suddenly began to roll down... and there he was, in all his magnificence! The hair, the smile, the eyeliner... and the voice yelling, "Well, God bless you, David! It's a pleasure to meet you!" I was completely at a loss for words. He inquired if I was a musician, the name of my band, and where I was from, all while signing a postcard-sized black-and-white photo of himself and writing, To David, God cares. We exchanged handshakes, the window opened, and my life was complete. I cannot emphasise how important these moments are to me. I'm like a small child in a museum, walking through this wild world of a musician, surrounded by the things I've spent a lifetime studying. And I am grateful when I finally meet someone who has inspired me along the way. I am thankful. And I don't take any of it for granted. I am a firm believer in music's shared humanity, which I find more fulfilling than any other component of my work. When a one-dimensional image transforms into a living, breathing, three-dimensional human being, it fills your soul with hope that even our most beloved heroes are made of flesh and bone. I believe that people inspire others. That is why, when my admirers approach me, I feel the desire to connect with them. I, too, am a fan.

My elder stoner cousin handed me his copy of Rush's magnum opus, 2112, when I was seven years old to take back to Virginia after our yearly vacation in Chicago. At the time, I was mostly listening to Beatles and KISS records, so Rush's prog rock skill and mastery were a whole new universe to my inexperienced ears. I was piqued. But it was the percussion on that album that really stuck out to me. It was the first time I'd heard them in the forefront of a song, as poetic and melodious as the vocals or guitar. I couldn't play what Neil Peart was doing, but I could FEEL it. Taylor Hawkins and I were requested to induct Rush into the Rock and Roll Hall of Fame and to perform the opening tune on 2112, an instrumental named "Overture" (no easy task). I'd met bassist Geddy Lee and guitarist Alex Lifeson throughout the years, both of whom were totally down-to-earth and outrageously funny, but never Neil Peart. Neil was more elusive, which was fair given that he was one of the greatest drummers of all time (not just in rock). Geddy and Alex greeted Taylor and me at rehearsal the day before the ceremony, but Neil was nowhere to be found. Then, in an instant, he emerged and said, in his rich baritone voice, "Hey, Dave, I'm Neil." All I could think about was when He spoke my name. He mentioned MY name. I greeted him cautiously, and he asked, "Would you like a coffee?" "Sure!" I said, and we walked over to the catering table, where he, Neil Peart, drummer of Rush, the man who inspired me to become a drummer at the age of seven, proceeded to make me a cup of coffee, giving it over with a smile. YET AGAIN, I AM INSPIRED.

It's one thing to see your idols in a musical setting or context; it's quite another to see them in their natural habitat, like an animal in the wild, far away from the spotlight. Elton John strolled out of a boutique directly in front of us and jumped in a waiting car once, as I was pushing Violet in a stroller down a busy London shopping street with my wife and our dear friend Dave Koz. We all came to a halt and exclaimed, "HOLY SHIT! OH MY GOD, DID YOU JUST SEE THAT?!?!?" It was Elton John. Fucking. John. And he was sitting in a parked car barely a few feet away, star struck. "Go say hi, Dave!" my pal nudged me. "I don't fucking know Elton John!" I laughed. And he has absolutely no idea who I am!" The automobile began, travelled about twenty metres up the road, and then stopped. Elton John stepped back to us, still frozen in place, as the door opened. He approached me and said, "Hello, Dave, nice to meet you." My smile was so big it almost slipped off my face. When I introduced him to Jordyn and Dave, he leaned down and kissed Violet before racing back and speeding away. That's how you do things, I reasoned. (And, yes, his massive sapphire earrings absolutely complemented his shoes.)

Years later, I was given the opportunity to play drums on a tune with Elton on the Queens of the Stone Age album... The song, "Fairweather Friends," was a furious, unorthodox multipart composition that we had meticulously rehearsed before his visit, because Queens usually recorded full band live to tape, which meant you had to have your shit together and get it right. Elton arrived, fresh off a session with Engelbert Humperdinck (no joke), and remarked, "Okay, boys, what?... "Do you have a ballad for me?" We all laughed and exclaimed, "No... Come listen." It would be impossible for anyone to walk in and learn such a hard song right away, but Elton sat at the piano and WORKED on it until he got it right, take after take, ever the perfectionist, proving why he is the queen bitch of rock and roll. YET AGAIN, I AM INSPIRED. It's the moments with no safety net that keep your spirits up, and if you're an explorer like me, you can always find those moments. And most of the time in the most unexpected places. Our tour manager, Gus, informed us one night in Osaka that Huey Lewis would be attending the show. "HUEY LEWIS!!!" Pat exclaimed loudly. I had never seen him so animated in all my years of knowing him. Pat utterly demolished my idea of him as the punkest motherfucker on the earth by informing me that the album Sports by Huey Lewis and the News was one of his favourite recordings of all time (along with Butterfly by Mariah Carey). Taylor then informed me that Huey actually played harmonica on Thin Lizzy's Live and Dangerous record, which I had no idea about but now makes sense. Huey emerged, and the backstage was soon buzzing with our regular beer and whiskey pre-show ritual. Take it from me, Huey is a fantastic hang. We drank, smoked, and laughed, and I ultimately inquired about his relationship with Phil Lynott and Thin Lizzy (great band). He told me about his harmonica solo on that song and how he, too, was a fan of Thin Lizzy. Then I had an idea: what if Huey stood up and joined us for a harmonica solo? He searched his pockets for a harp but found none, though he did say, "If you can find one in time, I'll do it!" I looked at the time; we had twenty minutes, so I turned to Gus and begged him to do whatever he could to find one, then performed one more shot with Huey before taking the stage. By the fifth song, I noticed Huey, beaming and waving his harp in the air. He hopped out next to me and started to shred a solo with a plastic harmonica purchased from a Japanese toy store on a Sunday night that would make the man from Blues Traveler throw down his bandoliers and flee to his mama. I was completely taken aback. This dude is a grade A, 100 percent badass motherfucker, and I will never again question the legitimacy of Sports. I'm sorry. For one night only, we were "Huey Lewis and the Foos," and I enjoyed it. ANOTHER TURN IN A PREVIOUSLY WINDING PATH.

You never know who might come on the side of the stage, so strike while the iron is hot. Years ago, the BBC requested us to record a cover song, which we like and do frequently, building a repertoire of tunes you never imagined you'd hear the Foo Fighters play (or attempt to do). We were on tour at the time, but we were supposed to record it as soon as we got back home, so we had to pick a song and have it ready to go within a few days. Taylor and I sat in our tiny warm-up area backstage at Tokyo's Summer Sonic music event, playing around with a few ideas, when I discovered Rick Astley was also on the list. "Dude, we should do 'Never Gonna Give You Up' for the BBC thing!" We started playing around with it, and I quickly noticed that the chord progression and arrangement sounded exactly like "Smells Like Teen Spirit." Pat, Chris, Rami, our keyboardist, and Nate joined in, and before long, the two tunes were virtually indistinguishable, like a hellish mash-up. It was so hilarious and absurd that we did it again and again, until Gus walked in and informed us it was time for the show. We took the enormous stadium stage and launched into our regular barn burner set, but after a few songs, I noticed a familiar figure by the monitor board stage right. It was Rick fucking Astley, rocking out to the band in the distance, his unmistakable boyish face bobbing up and down. I approached Rami and offered my hand during one of his keyboard solos. "We just learned 'Never Gonna Give You Up' half an hour ago," I remarked over the crushing noise of the show going on behind me. "Would you like to join us?" He was stunned but responded without hesitation, "Fuck yes," and within seconds he was onstage singing with a slew of strangers in front of fifty thousand puzzled Japanese Foo Fighters fans, flying by the seat of his trousers. Rick Astley, may God bless you. That took a lot of guts. Meeting a musician who has inspired you is not the same as meeting a musician who has no personal relevance in your life. That's an intriguing juxtaposition. Whereas I've melted into a puddle when I've met the most obscure, unknown, underground hardcore musicians, I've also been as cool as a cucumber when I've met luminaries whose music never became a part of my vocabulary. Not to suggest Neil Diamond isn't a god among men, but the "Sweet Caroline" single wasn't on my Venom and Dead Kennedys records as a kid, so when we met at the 2009 MusiCares tribute, where he was being recognized, I just thought he was a really nice guy. But there was one person I knew would melt into a puddle upon seeing him, and that was the mother of my late buddy Jimmy Swanson. And she was the reason we were there.

Mary Jane was a lifelong Neil Diamond lover, and save the screeching satanic death metal Jimmy and I listened to, this was probably the only music I ever heard at her house. She was utterly sad after Jimmy died, having lost her only son far too soon. She was like another mother to me, so when we were invited to sing a Neil Diamond song at his memorial, I replied, "Let me make one call before saying yes." I called Mary Jane and informed her that I would only play the show if she flew out to California for the first time to meet Neil. I called my boss and informed him everything was a go, and I started looking for a Neil Diamond song to learn, my first dive into his enormous collection. That weekend, I was on double duty, playing drums for Paul McCartney at the Grammys, where we blasted through a wonderfully raw version of "I Saw Her Standing There," so Mary Jane flew out and joined us, going from sitting on the couch in her TV room to sitting in an arena with Kid Rock, U2, and Stevie Wonder. We attended an after-party with Paul and the band that night at a restaurant, and when Mary Jane walked in, Paul brought her a glass of champagne, kissed her on the cheek, and said, "Hello, luv." I was afraid she was going to pass out. But it was the moment Paul stood up at the far end of the table to make a toast that still makes me cry. After toasting everyone in the room and the magnificent night of music we had just witnessed, Paul turned to Mary Jane and said, "And... to Jimmy."

The following night was Mary Jane's great chance to finally meet her idol, Neil Diamond. I had met him earlier in the day backstage, and he was a vision of seventies cool, with his red silk shirt with diamonds embroidered on the collar (which we all congratulated him on), immaculate hair, and a voice that would make anyone weak in the knees. I explained the emotional significance of the occasion, and he graciously agreed to come say hello to Mary Jane after the show.

I recall her expression when he entered our changing room later that night. I must have made the same expression when I met Little Richard, Paul, or any of the obscure, unknown, underground performers I admired. The point at when the one-dimensional becomes three-dimensional and you are reminded that the noises that have brought you joy, escape, and solace all began with flesh and bone. I could only see Jimmy crying tears of pleasure as Mary Jane did.

And the next day, Mary Jane went back to Virginia, carefully packing that red silk shirt with diamonds embroidered on the collar in her suitcase. Neil Diamond had, indeed, given her the shirt off his back.

Why are these people so important to me? Because people inspire others, and they have all become a part of my DNA throughout the years. Each and every note I've heard them play has shaped me in some manner. My memories have been painted with their voices as the frame. I recall my uncle Tom taking me sailing when I was a kid, and we spent the day listening to—you guessed it—"Sailing" by Christopher Cross. If this hadn't been such a formative experience, I might not have tackled a terrified Christopher Cross at the Austin, Texas, airport baggage claim one day just to see him in person. Or the time I approached Ace Frehley of KISS on a Hollywood street corner late at night for a simple handshake, or shyly proclaimed my love to Bonnie Raitt as we sat on the Rock and Roll Hall of Fame's dressing room floor. BECAUSE I STILL WALK THROUGH LIFE LIKE A LITTLE BOY IN A MUSEUM, SURROUNDED BY THE EXHIBITS I'VE SPENT A LIFETIME STUDYING, AND I AM THANKFUL WHEN I FINALLY COME FACE-TO-FACE WITH SOMETHING OR SOMEONE WHO HAS INSPIRED ME ALONG THE WAY. I AM THANKFUL.

But meeting a hero in passing is one thing. It's quite another when they become your friend.

I was walking toward the restroom of the seedy bar we were currently destroying with my crew years ago in Los Angeles when I noticed the one and only Lemmy sitting in the corner, drinking alone in front of a video poker machine (I won't say his last name or band affiliation because if you don't already know, then I have to break up with you). I couldn't help myself. This man was the live, breathing embodiment of rock & roll, and I had admired him since the first time I heard his gravelly voice blasting through my speakers. "Excuse me, Lemmy?" I said as I approached him. I just wanted to thank you for all of your years of inspiration." "Cheers," he hissed from beneath his black cowboy hat, in a thick cloud of Marlboro smoke. I was going to turn and walk away when he replied, "Sorry 'bout your friend Kurt."

Lemmy was no longer a globally revered rock and roll god after that; he was a fellow human being. We became friends over hundreds of smokes and bottles of Jack Daniel's throughout the years, swapping gruesome tales of life on the road and a mutual love of Little Richard. I admired his honesty, candour, and strength, as well as his fragility. Whether it was bellying up to the bar at the Rainbow Bar and Grill on the Sunset Strip (his home away from home, so much so that once while I was drinking with him there, the waitress came up and delivered him his mail) or at his messy apartment down the street, I relished every moment in his company. Because I admired him not only as a musician, but also as a friend.

I was shocked to learn of his death. It had just been a few days since his seventieth birthday and a few weeks since his last performance. I had assumed he would outlive all of us. He followed a difficult path that most would not survive, and though it took its toll on him later in life, he had the vigour and spirit of a warrior. Lemmy would not give up until he had no choice but to surrender and rest.

I immediately rushed to a tattoo parlour and branded my left wrist with an ace of spades and the words "SHAKE YOUR BLOOD," a phrase from a song we'd written together years before. He was a passionate rock and roll fan who lived life to the fullest, two qualities we definitely shared.

I was asked to speak at his memorial service a week or two later, and while holding back tears, I told a few memories about our time together to the small church full of his closest friends. This was a bittersweet celebration of his life, because he had provided us all so much joy but was now leaving us to face life without his priceless friendship.

I stood, taking out the small black-and-white photo that Little Richard had autographed for me years before from my jacket pocket, and read the words of an old gospel hymn that Little Richard had once performed, "Precious Lord, Take My Hand."

I turned around and thanked Lemmy by placing the image on his altar.

I will be eternally grateful for the inspiration.

CONCLUSION
ANOTHER STEP IN THE CROSSWALK

"You okay, buddy?"

Slumped in my chair, I gave Chris a silent, reassuring nod as I sobbed, my muffled cries echoing in the awkward silence of our dressing room as the other guys quietly opened their wardrobe cases and changed their clothes behind me, still sweating from the three-hour show we had just played. After twenty years in a band, Pat, Nate, Taylor, Chris, and Rami had never seen their courageous leader, me, utterly break down in front of them. But I couldn't take it any longer. I needed to let go. In a cathartic moment, it was as if every feeling I had suppressed for the previous forty years burst through the levee inside of me, flooding into the concrete floor below. It wasn't that I couldn't walk but had continued on an exhaustive tour of 65 concerts where I had to be put onto a chair each night to perform, only to be hauled away afterwards like a broken theatre prop. It wasn't that I still felt the burning pain of the jagged titanium screws bored deep into my bones, which would serve as a sobering reminder of my weakness and fragility for the rest of my life. And it wasn't because I was overcome with the agonising need for my family that tears my heart when we're apart for weeks on end, preying on my fear of absence and the separation anxiety left behind by my father. This was something else entirely. It was the fact that I had just finished playing a sold-out gig to forty thousand people at Chicago's Wrigley Field, exactly across the street from the Cubby Bear, the tiny club where I watched my first concert when I was thirteen and was motivated to commit my life to rock and roll.

I'd played stadiums twice this size before, leading a sea of people in chorus after chorus, all of us joining in joyous unison for hours, but it wasn't the sheer immensity of the place that had me in tears on this night. That dimly lit corner pub previously packed with bodies writhing and dancing to the deafening shriek of feedback and smashing drums served as my morning. My baptism was that July night in 1982, when my cousin Tracey took me to see Naked Raygun; I was immersed in the distorted splendour of the music. I was changed from that day forward, emboldened by the revelation I felt as my skinny little chest was smashed against the tiny stage and I was confronted with the raw power of rock and roll. I had finally discovered my specialty, tribe, and calling. But, most importantly, I had discovered myself. This was my profound awakening, and dreams became more than just dreams; they became my divining rod. I was an idealistic outcast, fueled by faith's daring and a reckless drive to do things on my own. Punk music became my professor in a school with no rules, just teaching the lesson that there are no courses and that everyone, regardless of sound, has a voice that should be heard. I've created a life on this idea and have blindly pursued it with unwavering belief. I had stepped out onto that crossing that night, and there was no turning back.

As the band filed out of the dressing room silently, I was left alone in my chair to contemplate and gently fit together the jagged pieces of this lifelong puzzle. I remembered lengthy trips in our old 1976 Ford Maverick car, singing along to AM radio, where I first heard the sound of two voices in harmony producing a chord. This was the spark that kindled my interest in music. I remembered the beautiful instrumental ferocity of Edgar Winter's "Frankenstein," my first album, which I bought at a drugstore and played on the record player my mother brought home from school until the needle wore out. I remembered the Silvertone guitar with the built-in amp that I used to play every day after school, strumming along to my Beatles songbook and learning the art of songwriting and arrangement. And I remembered the old pillows I used as drums on my bedroom floor, thrashing to my favourite punk rock recordings until my hands were bloodied. Each tear brings back another memory. Each recollection represents another step in the crosswalk.

Maybe my séance was successful after all. It had been thirty years since I knelt before the flickering candles of the altar I'd built in my carport and prayed to the universe for this blessing. Perhaps it was all a matter of generating desire, of thinking that everything is possible if you devote yourself completely to it. Perhaps it was the courage of believing in oneself. Perhaps I had sold my soul. All of this could be true, but I knew that if it hadn't been for the epiphany I had that night at the Cubby Bear, I would never have dared to attempt.

I would never have taken the opportunity and called my favourite local band, Scream, to audition, setting off a chain of events that would change my life forever. I would have taken a completely different path if I hadn't seen that flyer on the bulletin board at my local music store, but instead of staying in the comfort of my tiny bedroom, I decided to jump through it, leaving a life of stability and security behind. I was ready to be free, despite the fact that I was still linked to my youth. I was willing to stake everything on this raging passion inside of me, and I made a vow to honour it. Music had become my counsellor when I needed advice, my friend when I felt alone, my father when I needed love, my pastor when I needed hope, and my lover when I needed to belong when I was seventeen years old. When I witnessed the B-52s dance their crap around on Saturday Night Live in a weird, hyperactive blur, I felt a connection and realised I would never live a regular existence. I wasn't destined to become just another trench coat at the bus stop on the calm suburban streets of Springfield, Virginia. I was created to fly my freak flag and appreciate all of life's wonderful idiosyncrasies. I needed to deviate from the norm.

Another memory, another crosswalk step.

I was let go with my mother's approval. She recognized my purpose and gave me the opportunity to go as far as I wanted thanks to her boundless empathy and compassion. Life quickly became a survival lesson, and my house was a hard floor, but I was LIVING, and music became my nourishment when there was none to eat. I learned to surrender to the unpredictability of a life without design, to rely on a road map with no destination, letting it take me wherever it might lead, never knowing what was around the next corner but faithfully relying on the music to keep me alive in the event that everything fell apart and I had to start over.

And I did start over.

It seemed like only yesterday that I'd spent those long nights in Olympia, Washington, snuggled away in my sleeping bag thousands of miles away, waiting for my next dream. I was once again a stranger in a stranger's home, but the ringing in my ears from the sound we produced together in that little barn outside of town lulled me to sleep each night and kept my fire going. My trusty divining rod had led me to yet another well, this time one so deep that it eventually overflowed and drowned us all. I was stranded without a lifeboat.

I could have drowned. I had the option of giving up. I could have returned home. But giving up was never in my blood.

I composed myself and prepared to join the customary stream of after-show guests as I heard the room next door begin to fill. I could hear their voices and recognized all of them. These were the voices of the people who had helped me get through these difficult years. My new tribe consists of an extended family.

I walked into the room and saw Gus Brandt, who was handing people drinks and passes and doing his best to make everyone feel welcome in our chaotic little world. Gus had taken care of me for decades, part therapist, half big brother, part bodyguard, from broken guitars to shattered limbs. He'd become my beacon when I felt lost in a sea of strangers, my refuge when I needed it, and I could always confide in him about my deepest agony. Though he was not a musician, his passion for music was as strong as, if not stronger than, mine, and without his shoulder to lean on, I would never make it to the next song, city, or stage. He is always present, and I am grateful for his safety.

Rami Jaffee, my constant confidant, was floating around the room with the ease and nonchalance of a gypsy maître d', spreading his aura as the Foo Fighters' true "good times" ambassador. Though he was tucked away in the corner of the stage every night, his contribution to the band had proven vital over the years, and he had contributed an aspect of musicianship that had elevated us to another level record after album. But, aside from his musical ability, his companionship had become a source of joy every day, a welcome respite from the routine of life on the road. And each night, once the curtains have closed and the crowd has gone home, Rami and I will board our shared tour bus and drink, smoke, and dance our way down the highway to our next stop. Though he joined the band a decade later, he was one of us from the beginning, and I am grateful for his support.

There was Chris Shiflett, the man who rescued our band when we were without a guitarist and in severe need of musical assistance. Though our paths had crossed coincidentally ten years before his fateful audition (the only time we had ever attempted such a thing), we had lived parallel lives up until that point, playing in punk rock bands with friends and living out of vans on pennies, with music and adventure being the only real rewards. I knew he would fit in wonderfully before he had played a note because he would love every second of being in this band, and I am grateful for his gratitude.

Taylor Hawkins, my brother from another mother, my dearest friend, a man for whom I would take a bullet, ripped through the room like an F5 tornado of hyperactive delight. Our kinship was instant when we first met, and we got closer with every day, every song, and every note we ever played together. I'm not embarrassed to declare that our fortuitous meeting was love at first sight, lighting a musical "twin flame" that continues to burn to this day. We've become an irrepressible duo, both onstage and off, in search of any and every adventure we can find. We were born to be together, and I am thankful that we met in this lifetime.

Nate Mendel was my voice of reason, my barometer, the one I could always come to when I needed to be grounded. The world would never have known the Foo Fighters of today if it hadn't been for that chance encounter at my Thanksgiving meal in 1994, hunched around a Ouija board to contact the spirits of my haunted house in Seattle. We had constructed this monster together from the ground up, overcome numerous challenges, and stayed reasonably unscathed. Though I rarely express it, his presence in my life is essential, and I don't know what I would do without him. I appreciate his dedication and loyalty.

Pat Smear was another. The man who was once my punk rock hero and who became not only a bandmate twice over, but also a reliable pillar in my life. Pat was always there to walk through the fire with me, no matter the highs or lows, from the moment he walked into Nirvana's rehearsal space in 1993 and gave the band another year of life. He was always present for my life's most difficult struggles, and his wisdom and wit reassured me that I could get through anything.

That WE were capable of overcoming any obstacle. I hoped we'd be shoulder to shoulder from the first time we met, and I've been content to stand in his shadow ever since. Every night onstage, when I glance to my left and see heavy plumes of smoke streaming from his smile, I feel safe, and I will be eternally grateful for his kind and wise spirit.

We'd each turned into a whirring wheel in a deafening clock, only ticking when the spinning teeth of one gear met those of another, locking us into synchronised movement. Without it, our pendulum would come to a halt. The revolving door that had previously plagued our childhood had now been shut, and we had become a permanent thing. Once you're in, you're in for the long haul. The stability and security that we had all desired as children of divorce and adolescent rebellion might now be found in a bombardment of distorted guitars and laser-lit stages. We'd grown into a family.

Jordyn, the mother of my children, the queen of my world, the weight in my scale that stops the arm from tipping, was holding court in the far corner of the room with a glass of champagne in her exquisite palm. Our paths had met at a moment when I feared I was doomed to live forever in the past, but she showed me a future through her courage and clarity. We created my life's greatest achievement, my family, together. And, as our family expanded, so did my appreciation for life. I was born again with each child, and with each step they took, I retraced my own. In exchange, Violet, Harper, and Ophelia gave me life, and words cannot explain how grateful I am to them. Fatherhood trumped every hope, wish, or song I'd ever written, and as the years passed, I learned the true meaning of love. I don't simply live for myself anymore; I live for them.

The voices that could not be heard, however, were possibly the loudest in the room.

Jimmy should've been here, I reasoned. When I returned home from Chicago in 1982, he was the first person I played my Naked Raygun record for, and the instant we dropped the needle on that primitive slab of vinyl, we went on a new musical journey together as allies in the unconventional world of punk rock. We were two outcasts in a sea of uniformity who, through our fixation with music, formed our own world, language, and cosmos. No matter how far off I was, he always understood me and accepted my oddity, just as I accepted his. I looked up to him as the older brother I never had, and he shaped so much of who I am. We had been intertwined our entire lives, sharing everything, and it hurt my heart that I couldn't enjoy this moment with him. But I knew deep down that he would have cherished this win since it belonged to both of us.

"This will never last," my father once warned me, and it's possible that it was this challenge that motivated me to make it last. We had fought to connect our entire lives, yet even in his absence, his presence impacted me, for better or worse. I had long since let go of any bitterness toward him and had forgiven him for his mistakes as a parent, easing the strain of our relationship and allowing us to become wonderful friends. I had received more than just fundamental physical characteristics from him as his child: we had the same hands, knees, and arms. I have to think that my talent to discern sound and perform music by ear was passed down from his wonderful genetic code, and that I owed this most valuable gift to him. Something he undoubtedly noticed as I grew older.

I know he'd be proud, and I wish dad was still here to complete this cycle with me.

Kurt as well.

If he could have seen the joy that his music provided to the world, he might have discovered his own. Kurt impacted my life forever, something I never had the opportunity to express while he was still with us, and not thanking him for that is a regret I will have to live with until we are reunited. I don't go a day without thinking about our time together, and when we meet in my dreams, there's always a sense of happiness and peace, almost as if he's only been hiding, waiting to return.

Though they are no longer with us, I carry these individuals with me wherever I go, just as they once carried me, and it is their faces that I see every night just before the house lights go out and I am greeted by a scream of applause. It is theirs just as much as it is mine. I imagined that if they had just hung on a little longer, they might have joined in this celebration, another reunion of lifetime friends bonded by years of deep connection.

But in the midst of it all stood the unmistakable matriarch of this extended family, the person to whom all forty thousand screaming fans had just sung "Happy Birthday" earlier that night: my mother. I was overcome with emotion as she stood on the stage beside me while the entire stadium rang out in thunderous chorus, knowing that this woman who had worked tirelessly to raise two children on her own—struggling to make ends meet, working multiple jobs, living paycheck to paycheck—and devoted her entire life to the benefit of others as a public school teacher was finally getting the recognition she deserved. It goes without saying that without her, none of us would have been there. She had given me life not once, but twice, by allowing me to be who I wanted to be and, in the end, by releasing me to my own fate. She gave me the guts and confidence to believe in myself because she believed in me. She taught me to live with passion and conviction. And she taught me how to love others unconditionally via her unconditional love for me. She had the option of giving up. She may have returned home. Surrender, on the other hand, was never in her DNA.

She will always be my hero and biggest inspiration; I owe everything to her.

It had taken a lifetime to get to that crosswalk, but I was grateful for every step, still that same little boy with a guitar and a dream. Because I still don't realise I'm getting older. My thoughts and emotions continue to play this terrible joke on me, tricking me with the illusion of youth as I greet the world every day through the idealistic, mischievous eyes of a rebellious child who is always on the lookout for adventure and magic. I still find delight and gratitude in the simplest of things. And as I accumulate more lines and scars, I still wear them with pride, as they nearly act as a trail of breadcrumbs thrown across a route that I will someday rely on to find my way back to where I started.

My tears had now dried, and I gently entered the room on my two broken crutches, only to be greeted by a massive communal embrace. The circle had been completed, and we had all crossed the street together, glad for life, music, and the people we care about.

AND SUCCESS.

The contents of this book may not be copied, reproduced or transmitted without the express written permission of the author or publisher. Under no circumstances will the publisher or author be responsible or liable for any damages, compensation or monetary loss arising from the information contained in this book, whether directly or indirectly. .

Disclaimer Notice:

Although the author and publisher have made every effort to ensure the accuracy and completeness of the content, they do not, however, make any representations or warranties as to the accuracy, completeness, or reliability of the content. , suitability or availability of the information, products, services or related graphics contained in the book for any purpose. Readers are solely responsible for their use of the information contained in this book

Every effort has been made to make this book possible. If any omission or error has occurred unintentionally, the author and publisher will be happy to acknowledge it in upcoming versions.

Copyright © 2023

All rights reserved.

Printed in Great Britain
by Amazon